YORK NOTES

THE PARDONER'S TALE

GEOFFREY CHAUCER

NOTES BY SHAUN McCARTHY

 Longman

 York Press

The right of Shaun McCarthy to be identified as Author of this Work has been asserted
by him in accordance with the Copyright, Designs and Patents Act 1988

YORK PRESS
322 Old Brompton Road, London SW5 9JH

PEARSON EDUCATION LIMITED
Edinburgh Gate, Harlow,
Essex CM20 2JE, United Kingdom
Associated companies, branches and representatives throughout the world

First published 2008
Fourth impression 2011

ISBN 978–1–4058–9620–7

Phototypeset by Pantek Arts Ltd, Maidstone, Kent

Printed in China (EPC/04)

CONTENTS

PART ONE
INTRODUCTION

Studying verse narratives 5

Reading *The Pardoner's Tale* 6

PART TWO
THE TEXT

Note on the text 12

Synopsis 13

Detailed summaries

The Pardoner in *The General Prologue* 15

The Introduction to *The Pardoner's Tale* 20

The Pardoner's Prologue 24

The Pardoner's Tale 40

Extended commentaries

Text 1: *The Pardoner's Prologue* (lines 43–90) 73

Text 2: *The Pardoner's Tale* (lines 263–302) 74

Text 3: *The Pardoner's Tale* (lines 520–64) 76

PART THREE
CRITICAL APPROACHES

Characterisation 78

Themes

Deception.. 86

Corruption 87

Gluttony and drunkenness... 89

Religion and dissent.. 90

Avarice and the abuse of power.................................... 92

Death 93

Structure 94

Confession, sermon and moral tale 94

Narrative techniques

Chaucer's authorial position 96

Language and style
Chaucer's English **99**
The poetry of *The Canterbury Tales* **100**
The voices of *The Pardoner's Tale* **100**
Imagery **101**
Allusion **103**
Rhetoric **105**

PART FOUR
CRITICAL PERSPECTIVES

Reading critically **107**
Original reception **107**
Later criticism **108**
Contemporary approaches **109**
Marxist criticism **109**
Humanist criticism **110**
Dramatic criticism **111**

PART FIVE
BACKGROUND

Geoffrey Chaucer's life and works **112**
Chaucer's other works **114**
Literary background
The gothic tradition in literature **118**
Verse narratives **121**
Chaucer and other writers **122**
Historical background **123**
Chronology **127**

FURTHER READING **132**

LITERARY TERMS **136**

AUTHOR OF THESE NOTES **139**

PART ONE

INTRODUCTION

STUDYING VERSE NARRATIVES

Reading verse narratives and exploring them critically can be approached in a number of ways, but when reading the text for the first time it is a good idea to consider some, or all, of the following:

- **Format and style:** how do verse narratives differ from other genres of text? How are stanzas or other divisions used to reveal information, and how do the characters or voices convey emotion?

- **The writer's perspective:** consider what the writer has to say, how he or she presents a particular view of people, the world, society, ideas, issues, etc. Are, or were, these views controversial?

- **Shape and structure:** explore the relationship between the main narrative and any subsidiary ones. How do these narratives develop through revelation and reflection, conflicts and resolutions?

- **Choice of language:** does the writer choose to write formally or informally? Does he or she use different registers for characters, voices or groups, vary the sound and style, or employ language features such as **imagery** and dialect?

- **Verse and metre:** What rhythms and rhymes does the writer use to create pace and interest, convey an atmosphere or achieve an effect?

- **Links and connections:** what other texts does this verse narrative remind you of? Can you see connections between its narrative, main voices, characters and ideas and those of other texts you have studied? Is the poem part of a literary movement or tradition?

- **Your perspective and that of others:** what are your feelings about the verse narrative? Can you relate to the voices, characters, themes and ideas? What do others say about it – for example, critics or other writers?

These York Notes offer an introduction to *The Pardoner's Tale* and cannot substitute for close reading of the text and the study of secondary sources.

 CHECK THE BOOK

Other collections of individual tales told by a group of characters existed before Chaucer's *Canterbury Tales*, the most famous being the *Decameron* (1348–53), written by the Italian author Boccaccio. In this work, three lords and seven ladies hide from the plague in a country villa and while away the days telling stories.

READING *THE PARDONER'S TALE*

The Canterbury Tales is Geoffrey Chaucer's longest and certainly best-known work. He was still writing it when he died in 1400. If he had completed his overall plan – that each of the twenty-nine pilgrims would tell two Tales on the way to Canterbury and two on the return journey – he would have created a huge collection of a hundred and sixteen Tales. In fact, he completed just twenty-two. Nonetheless, together they present a vast panorama of life and characters from the late 1300s. Of the Tales Chaucer completed, *The Pardoner's Tale* is one of the best known and most studied. The actual Tale the Pardoner tells to the pilgrims, a moral story about three sinful young men, is relatively short and simple. It is the way that Chaucer creates the character of the Pardoner that is remarkable. Writers in the Middle Ages didn't usually explore personality and motive in such depth, nor do so through the character's own words. Scholars agree that the Pardoner is the most complex and fully-realised character in the whole of *The Canterbury Tales*.

Despite a lack of definite 'dates and details', we know enough to see that Chaucer's life was in many ways like *The Canterbury Tales*: varied and busy. He was born a 'commoner' into a rigorously hierarchical society, probably in 1343. However, there were sufficient family connections to the ruling aristocratic class – his father and grandfather had held minor positions in the royal court – for Chaucer to move with relative ease above his lowly position. His first recorded employment was in a noble household, working in some unspecified capacity for the Countess of Ulster. At the age of twenty-two he married a woman from a higher social class. He held various official positions of considerable authority at different times of his life. He also suffered periods of extreme poverty, and served for a year (1359–60) with the English army fighting in France (see **Background: Geoffrey Chaucer's life and works**).

Throughout his life, Chaucer moved through different levels of society. His experiences allowed him to create a wide range of characters for *The Canterbury Tales*: the aristocratic Knight, the bawdy Miller, and, one of his most vivid and potentially controversial creations, the cheating, hypocritical Pardoner. Chaucer's great creative imagination allowed him to bring all these diverse characters vividly to life. Unlike the Italian author Boccaccio who created only aristocratic characters for his collection of tales, the *Decameron*, Chaucer creates aristocrats as easily as he brings to life people like the Pardoner, who is little better than a common trickster.

What gave Chaucer such freedom to move through the various layers of the strictly hierarchical society in which he lived was his knowledge of many different subjects (sciences as well as arts) and his creative intelligence. He was probably one of the most widely-read men of his time. This is reflected in the variety of his works. He created great verse narratives such as *The Canterbury Tales*, full of bawdy humour and earthy vitality. He wrote the highly stylised *Troilus and Criseyde*. He translated poetry and prose from the French, Latin and Italian. He wrote essays on subjects such as medicine, astronomy, astrology, the law and alchemy. He used his extensive knowledge in many of his creative works, as demonstrated by the wide range of references and **allusions** he employs in *The Pardoner's Tale*.

Chaucer was not only diverse in the choice of subjects he chose to write about, he also employed a range of literary styles and conventions (see **Background: Geoffrey Chaucer's life and works**). Sometimes, as with *The Pardoner's Tale*, he employs two or more types of story structure in one work. In this Tale, Chaucer draws upon three distinct story structure elements: the confession, the **sermon** and the **moral tale**. He hangs all this around the development of the character of the Pardoner as he reveals himself to the pilgrims.

The Pardoner's Tale is important to modern readers for several reasons. It is a very accessible piece of writing once you overcome the problems of reading the language in which it is written. In fact,

---

CONTEXT

Alchemy was the chemistry of the Middle Ages, but it was a far less scientific study than chemistry. Alchemists were almost entirely preoccupied with finding a chemical way of turning 'base' or everyday metals into gold.

 CHECK THE BOOK

Troilus and Criseyde is Chaucer's other great work. It is very different from *The Canterbury Tales* and is a **courtly romance** set in classical times at the siege of Troy. It presents a chivalrous, idealised view of love and war.

CONTEXT

When tackling Chaucer's language, if the word order in a line of the text looks confusing, find the subject of the statement and try to put the other words in a different order around it. Chaucer inverts the sentence structure we would use – 'now you I tell' instead of 'now I tell you', for example.

CONTEXT

Chroniclers were writers who recorded events, often in the form of lists arranged by dates. Unlike historians, they did not usually attempt to compare, interpret or generalise historical events, and they often recorded only things that happened within their own lifetimes.

much of this difficulty lies in Chaucer's spelling, for example 'y's where we put 'e's, and 'e's on the ends of words. Some sentences also arrange words in a different order (what we call **syntax**) from the way in which we structure writing today. It is obviously easier to understand, appreciate and enjoy what Chaucer is saying if you are not constantly struggling with how he says it. The **Detailed summaries, Extended commentaries** and especially the glossaries in Part Two of these Notes will help you to get to grips with Chaucer's language. Once you can read back and forth through the text more fluently, you will find that it contains lively portraits of characters who are not so far removed from present-day life. Chaucer's extensive use of direct speech allows us to 'hear' their voices and this gives the work energy and immediacy. What the Pardoner sells and why people would be foolish enough to buy pardons and relics might seem remote and obscure to us, but today people are still tricked out of their money by fraudsters. Despite all sorts of warnings, some people still invest in schemes that offer unachievable profits. We might see in their misplaced faith in these financial schemes an echo of a medieval congregation's hopes of gaining exceptional spiritual rewards in return for donations.

In contrast to these elements, which appear timeless, Chaucer also offers a clear window on the many differences between his age and ours. Only a few works of literature were created when Chaucer was writing, or have survived for us to read. Historians and chroniclers did not generally record the vivid details of daily life that are included everywhere in Chaucer. As well as being a great work of creative literature, *The Canterbury Tales* provides us with a view of everyday medieval England.

The Canterbury Tales occupies a crucial position in the early history of English literature. Chaucer's works are the first major texts in Middle English along with those of his contemporaries William Langland, who wrote only one well-known text, *Piers Plowman*, and the unknown author of the Arthurian romance *Sir Gawain and the Green Knight*. The only significant surviving and still popular work of fiction created in (Old) English before

Chaucer is the anonymous poem *Beowulf*. Chaucer is therefore generally regarded as the most important writer before Shakespeare. Like Shakespeare, he often uses traditional stories as the basis for some of his own plots. Also, like Shakespeare, he uses his talents to take the bare bones of folk tales and develop them into full stories. The moral story told within *The Pardoner's Tale* is a perfect example of this.

The Canterbury Tales are important not just as the starting point for studying the later literature that they inspired, but as a way of looking back to folk tales and stories from other cultures and languages that Chaucer adapted and brilliantly developed in his own work. Many of these original tales and sources are lost to us: Chaucer's use of key elements of them in *The Canterbury Tales* allows us to gain a sense of the oral and **ballad** narrative traditions that preceded him. In a similar way, later authors, and contemporary film and television directors, have used different Tales as the basis for modern versions. It is a testament to the enduring quality of storytelling and characterisation in *The Canterbury Tales* that some of these modern versions keep fairly closely to the plot and characterisation of Chaucer's original story. The BBC made a modern day version of *The Pardoner's Tale* for its 2003 selection of *Canterbury Tales*.

Chaucer can also be described as a **gothic** author. In its widest sense, the term 'gothic' means a style of writing or, more often, of architecture and design, originating in the Middle Ages and distinct from classical style, which derives from ancient Greece and Rome. Chaucer is therefore gothic himself because he was writing in the Middle Ages. However, gothic more commonly describes writing with a particular emphasis on the macabre and an intention to repel and chill. In the study of literature, gothic often refers to a type of early novel, characterised by supernatural horror and by a focus on darkness and creating terror. *Frankenstein* (Mary Shelley, 1818) and *Dracula* (Bram Stoker, 1897) are probably the two best-known prose works of gothic literature. Early plays with supernatural events at their core are also considered gothic: Shakespeare's *Macbeth* (1603) with its witches, and Marlowe's *Dr Faustus* (1604)

CHECK THE BOOK

The best-known surviving example of a medieval chronicle is *The Anglo-Saxon Chronicle*, compiled by monks in different monastic institutions (mainly in Winchester, Canterbury and Peterborough) recording events in England from the arrival and spread of Christianity in the early ninth century to the middle of the twelfth century.

CHECK THE BOOK

Beowulf: A New Verse Translation by Seamus Heaney (Faber, 1999) is a vivid modern language verse translation of the poem with the original Old English text included.

CONTEXT

Middle English developed from Old English or Anglo-Saxon between 1100 and 1150 and lasted until about 1500 when Modern English developed. The spread of Modern English was accelerated by the growing availability of printed texts after 1470.

where a man sells his soul to the devil and is finally taken down to hell, are masterpieces of drama with gothic elements. In this sense, *The Pardoner's Tale* is a strongly gothic text, with its repellent descriptions of the destructive effects of committing sins, the Pardoner's macabre trade in bones and relics and the mysterious and dark figure of the Old Man.

It is important to remember that *The Pardoner's Tale* is a work of creative fiction. It was intended to be a popular work of entertainment, as far as any written work could be in an age when most people were illiterate and the printing press had not been invented. It is likely that if Chaucer were alive today he would be a writer of great stories featuring ordinary people. The characters within the Tales want to entertain their companions, and Chaucer wanted *The Canterbury Tales* to entertain his readers. He wanted them to laugh, be surprised, shocked and to be drawn into the world he creates of the pilgrims journeying in a fairly leisurely way along the road in the spring weather. It is a work primarily designed to amuse and excite: any deeper themes are secondary to this overall intention. In reading Chaucer it is important to see beyond the language difficulties to the simple storytelling and entertainment of the Tales.

CONTEXT

Unlike Shakespeare, who used source material for many of his plays taken from texts that still exist in written form, Chaucer's sources for some of *The Canterbury Tales* come from traditional folk tales. Versions of the Tale the Pardoner tells exist in oral traditions across Europe and even in India. Though these have since been recorded, no written texts survive dating from the Middle Ages.

The desire to entertain is reinforced by the lack of overt moral messages. Chaucer the author, and Chaucer the apparently mild-mannered and good-natured character in his Tales, does not push 'messages' or opinions at his readers. He presents characters and their stories and lets the readers make up their own minds about their moral worth, their bravery or lack of it, their good taste or their rough vulgarity, their piety or (in the case of the Pardoner) their lack of spiritual values. Despite the sometimes difficult language, and the passage of over seven hundred years between the world Chaucer knew and depicted and our own, there is much in *The Canterbury Tales* that seems fresh and relevant to us. This is because, perhaps above all else, Chaucer shows us what is eternal and unchanging in the human condition.

The following Notes aim to suggest key ways of approaching your own critical study of *The Pardoner's Tale*. The best approach to reading critically is to think about what you are reading, how it makes you feel, what ideas it connects with for you, and to then engage in original, personal interpretation of the text. A key part of this process is to form your own response to the Tale: what you like and dislike, what makes sense to you and what (at first) seems to pass you by. Reading around the subject to help you understand the social, moral, religious and cultural contexts in which Chaucer was writing is essential. You should find that researching the views of others and exploring your own reactions to the text is a perfect way to study this fascinating and lively Tale (for more on **Reading critically** see **Part Four**).

CHECK THE FILM

Italian director Pier Paulo Pasolini's film *The Canterbury Tales* (1971) is very loosely based on three of the Tales. He also made a film of Boccaccio's *Decameron* (1970), and one of tales from *The Arabian Nights* (1974).

THE TEXT

NOTE ON THE TEXT

Editors generally place *The Pardoner's Tale* about halfway through the sequence of Tales the pilgrims tell one another on their way from London to Canterbury. Printing had not been invented when Chaucer wrote *The Canterbury Tales* – it is usually thought that he started writing them in about 1387 – and all surviving copies from his lifetime are texts handwritten by scribes for customers who had different requirements. They apparently ordered small changes to be made to the copies specially written for them. There are approximately eighty-four surviving hand-produced early versions of *The Canterbury Tales*. This is a remarkably large number for a single medieval text and reflects the work's immediate popularity. Chaucer himself authenticated ten different versions of the text, though none are in his own hand.

The Tales were first printed in approximately 1478 by William Caxton, who many regard as being the first English printer to use a mechanical press. No two handwritten manuscripts are identical, and it is not clear in what order Chaucer himself wanted the stories to appear. *The Canterbury Tales* remained unfinished at the time of his death in 1400.

These Notes are based on the single edition of *The Pardoner's Prologue and Tale* edited by A. C. Spearing, published by the Cambridge University Press (most recent edition 2006). Other single editions of the Tale or complete editions of *The Canterbury Tales* may feature different spellings and other textual differences to the quotations given in these Notes.

SYNOPSIS

A group of pilgrims are travelling from the Tabard Inn in London to the shrine of St Thomas à Becket at Canterbury, telling tales as they go. They are accompanied by a figure called the Host, who is the landlord of the Tabard Inn.

INTRODUCTION TO *THE PARDONER'S TALE* (LINES 1–42)

The Host describes how the previous Tale (*The Physician's Tale*) has made him downhearted, with its tragic ending. He invites the Pardoner to cheer him up with a merry tale. The Pardoner agrees, but some of the more genteel pilgrims fear the Pardoner may come up with a bawdy story and they ask that he gives them a tale with a strong moral message.

THE PARDONER'S PROLOGUE (LINES 43–176)

The Pardoner takes great delight in telling the pilgrims how he preaches to simple congregations and country priests. He always bases his sermons on the same text from the Bible – namely that the 'love of money is the root of all evil'. He details the things he carries and has with him on the pilgrimage: letters of authority apparently written by powerful churchmen, and 'holy relics' that he admits are fakes. He says he extracts money from people and uses it to fund a good life for himself.

THE PARDONER'S TALE (LINES 177– 862)

The Tale begins with the Pardoner introducing his audience to a trio of young men drinking, gambling and swearing in a tavern in Flanders. They are habitual sinners. He breaks off before anything has actually happened to them to preach against the sins these men commit. He begins with drunkenness, and then turns his scorn on gluttony, where he uses very physical and graphic images to paint a disgusting picture of the effects of over-eating. He returns to attacking drunkenness again, then gambling. In this extended 'demonstration' sermon, the Pardoner is showing the pilgrims that he is an eloquent public speaker. Finally, at line 374, he says he will now 'telle forth my Tale'.

> **CONTEXT**
>
> Thomas à Becket (1118?–70) was murdered as he prayed in Canterbury Cathedral by three knights who claimed they were carrying out King Henry II's wishes. Becket and the king had rowed and the king had uttered hasty words that the knights had overheard, but he did not order Becket to be killed. Henry was grief-stricken and undertook regular penance at Thomas's shrine.

> **CONTEXT**
>
> Flanders was an independent country in Chaucer's time, centred on the city of Bruges (now in Belgium) and occupying lands that are now part of north-west Belgium, southern Holland and northern France.

CHECK THE BOOK

Nevill Coghill translated the complete *Canterbury Tales* into modern English in 1951 (Penguin Classics, 2003). His version of *The Pardoner's Tale* follows the A. C. Spearing/Cambridge University Press text closely, but not word for word. Nevertheless, reading Coghill's version alongside the original text will give you a good sense of how the *Prologue* and *Tale* are constructed.

The Tale moves on and now focuses on the three young men in the tavern who hear a funeral going by. They are told that the deceased was a friend of theirs who was killed the night before by a thief called 'Death'. They vow to find this villain Death and kill him. Soon after leaving the tavern they meet a mysterious Old Man. They treat him roughly, demanding to know if he knows where Death is. The Old Man complains that he has lived too long, that he has wandered the world trying to find someone to swap their youth for his age. When threatened by the young men, he says he saw Death not long ago, a little way off under a tree. The three men go to the tree and find not Death but a pile of gold coins. The 'worste' (490) of the young men says that they should draw lots for one of them to go into town to get food and drink. Then they will guard the treasure and move it to one of their homes after dark. The youngest of them draws the lot and he sets off.

As soon as he has gone, one of the two guarding the treasure suggests they kill the youngest when he comes back, and split the coins just two ways. Meanwhile the youngest thinks that if he could kill the other two, he could keep all the treasure for himself. In town, he buys poison and some empty bottles, two of which he fills with poisoned wine. The two who guarded the gold start a mock fight with their 'friend' when he returns, in the middle of which they stab him to death. They celebrate the success of their plan by drinking the poisoned wine and die. They have, as they claimed they would, found death, but it is their own (593–608).

The Pardoner further denounces the sins he preached against earlier. He shows the pilgrims how he would, after telling such a story to a congregation, encourage them to buy pardons. The Pardoner seems to forget that he has already said his pardons are worthless. He tells the pilgrims that they need to be in a State of Grace in case they meet any misfortunes on the road. He invites the Host to be first to buy a pardon. The moral tone of the Tale is completely undermined by the furious Host's vehement wish that he had the Pardoner's testicles in his hand, so he could cut them off. Although this is a vulgar, humorous comment, the Host is also introducing a sense of moral rectitude that sweeps away the Pardoner's attempt at deception. The Pardoner is struck dumb, and the pilgrims are laughing. The Knight steps in to make the Host and Pardoner kiss and order is restored.

DETAILED SUMMARIES
THE PARDONER IN *THE GENERAL PROLOGUE*

LINES 671–716

- Chaucer introduces the Pardoner last of all the pilgrims.
- The Pardoner's extraordinary appearance is depicted.
- The Pardoner's fake relics and his skill in selling them are also described.

 CHECK THE NET
Harvard University has a very large and useful site focused entirely on *The Pardoner's Tale.* Go to **www.courses.fas. harvard.edu/~ chaucer,** click on *The Canterbury Tales,* and then *Fragment VI.*

In *The General Prologue* Chaucer introduces the pilgrims in a strict descending order – from the most aristocratic, moral and spiritually virtuous to the most immoral and deceitful. The Pardoner is the last of the all the pilgrims to be introduced. Chaucer explains how the Pardoner makes his dishonest living and describes his strange and unpleasant physical appearance and mode of dress. However, Chaucer ends his description of the Pardoner in an even-handed way, by saying that despite his utter lack of moral scruples the Pardoner is a talented performer in church.

COMMENTARY

Chaucer uses *The General Prologue* to lay out his framework for the great collection of stories he is going to tell. The idea of a collection of diverse Tales told by a cast of twenty-nine characters with different voices and opinions was completely new to readers in the Middle Ages, though other authors had created smaller and less varied collections told by different voices. Chaucer needed his readers to understand the framework for the stories being told as this diverse group of pilgrims made their way from London to Canterbury and back.

Most of *The General Prologue* consists of a series of detailed descriptions of the appearance, employment and character of each of the pilgrims as they gather at the Tabard Inn in Southwark ready to set off on their pilgrimage. Together they present a complete and dynamic cross-section of medieval society – from the aristocratic Knight and his son the Squire, down through characters who are increasingly less wealthy and certainly less pious, moral and, in some cases, less honest. By the time Chaucer gets to the end of his descriptions, he has introduced some vulgar and brutish characters, and several habitual cheats.

It is therefore significant that he puts the Pardoner right at the end of his descriptions in *The General Prologue*. The implication is that he regards the Pardoner as being at the very bottom of the moral order. The Pardoner is put here because he cheats people by playing on their religious convictions. Chaucer, neither as the author nor as a character travelling along with the pilgrims, ever makes a direct personal critical statement about any of the characters. He merely presents their faults and leaves the readers to judge them. Committing fraud against poor people by abusing a lay position in the Church and their genuine religious beliefs would have been regarded as morally abhorrent by most of Chaucer's audience. We do not, however, anywhere gain an insight into how the Pardoner's words are being received by the pilgrims – apart from in their laughter at the Host's remarks at the end of the Tale.

Fraudulent pardoners were a common feature of life in medieval England and it may be that far from wanting to create in the Pardoner a person of utter moral degeneracy to be scorned, Chaucer was creating a character who both appalled the pilgrims and his readers but also made them laugh. Critics regard Chaucer as having a wide and deserved reputation as a comic writer: 'The phrase "a Canterbury Tale" has a long and popular association with laughter' (Pope, *How to Study Chaucer*, 2001, p. 179). The modern equivalent of the Pardoner might be an unscrupulous businessman whom we abhor as a realistic depiction of an unsavoury type drawn from real life, but at whom we also laugh for being an exaggerated comic figure who revels in his villainy.

CHECK THE BOOK

The Miller's Tale is probably the best-known of all *The Canterbury Tales*. It is the second story, after *The Knight's Tale*, which is by far the longest and most **courtly** in the collection. *The Miller's Tale* in contrast is about a gullible carpenter with a young wife who takes lovers, and has a horrible practical joke played on him involving a red-hot iron.

Chaucer's ranking of characters in *The General Prologue* is based on moral and spiritual values, not mere wealth or worldly position. The poor but genuinely pious Friar is described long before the Miller, who is clearly far better off materially, but some of whose wealth is derived from cheating customers. The cheating miller was a stock figure in many medieval stories.

Probably the kindest thing that is said about the Pardoner is in the first line of the description when Chaucer calls him 'gentil' (671). The image of the Pardoner and the Summoner singing together 'ful lowde' (674) may seem jolly and harmless, but then Chaucer describes the Pardoner as a man of grotesque appearance. His hair is 'yelwe' as wax and hangs over his shoulders in strands (676–80). Unusually for a man in Chaucer's time, the Pardoner has no beard, and the implication appears to be that he is incapable of growing one. He has bulging eyes, 'glarying eyyen' (686), like a hare and his voice is thin and reedy. Chaucer thinks that all this indicates that the Pardoner is in fact a eunuch, like a 'gelding' (693) – a gelding is a male horse which has been castrated.

To the late medieval mind, a man who was a eunuch was automatically depraved. Having one's testicles cut off does not, of course, lead to depravity, but Chaucer's audience generally believed it did. The implied accusation in all this is that the Pardoner is not only a cheat, he is, because of his physical condition (never actually confirmed in the Tales) inevitably morally corrupt. Chaucer leaves the idea for readers to ponder. Chaucer himself, as a character in his Tales, doesn't reveal how this possible fact about the Pardoner makes him feel.

Having made this insulting and damning suggestion about the Pardoner, Chaucer goes on to report how he is famous throughout the land (from Berwick on the Scottish borders to Ware, a town just north of London) for his skill and success in preaching and selling pardons and holy relics to gullible country parsons and their congregations. This is, in fact, further implied criticism, for Chaucer immediately goes on to describe how everything that the Pardoner sells is fake. He has a pillowcase in his bag that he claims is the veil of Mary Magdalene, and various pig's bones that he maintains are

CONTEXT

Eunuchs were men who had been deliberately castrated. In some Middle Eastern states they were employed as guards to harems. In Europe, up to the late eighteenth century, certain singing schools encouraged young boys to be castrated to maintain their high singing voices into adulthood. These singers were known as 'castrati'.

CONTEXT

Chaucer says that the Pardoner, though he is based at 'Rouncivale' (672) in London, 'streight was comen fro the court of Rome' (673), meaning the Vatican, heart of the Catholic Church. He does not comment on whether this might be true or not. It is probably a falsehood, the first sign of the Pardoner's deceptions, because even for devout and dedicated churchmen such overseas pilgrimages were difficult and rare events.

from the skeletons of saints. Chaucer doesn't say outright these are bogus, but he twice in quick succession (698–9) uses the phrase 'he seyde' and lists the real nature of the 'holy' objects. It is a very neat and slightly comic way of introducing the fact that the Pardoner is a peddler of worthless trash. However, holy relics were highly prized in Chaucer's time and the Pardoner makes a very good living for himself out of cheating people.

It is interesting to note that the penultimate character to be introduced in *The General Prologue*, just before the Pardoner, is the Summoner, another lay official of the Church. Summoners called people to attend church trials. It was not a profession that made them popular. The Summoner and the Pardoner share many qualities. Both approach their jobs with self-interest which compromises their moral standing; both have an unpleasant physical appearance. From the start of the pilgrimage, they appear to seek out one another's companionship on the road to Canterbury. Maybe this is as much because they know many of the other pilgrims will regard them with equal suspicion as because they share personal qualities. By putting two lay church officials at the bottom of the ordering of pilgrims by moral worth, Chaucer is clearly being personally critical – or at least reflecting popular opinion – of the general moral laxity of lay persons who worked for the Church.

CONTEXT

'Rouncivale' refers to the Augustinian hospital of St Mary of Roncesvalle, which was a genuine and respected religious institution in London that was selling pardons in the 1380s.

GLOSSARY

675	**stif burdoun** a strong singing accompaniment
676	**trompe** to trumpet loudly
677	**yelow as wex** yellow as wax
678	**flex** flax
680	**overspraddle** spread over
681	**colpons** long thin strands (of hair)
682	**jolitee** gaiety, light-heartedness
	wered he noon he did not wear (his hood)
683	**walet** a bag
684	**al of the newe jet** all of the new fashion
685	**he rood al bare** he rode bareheaded
686	**swiche** such
687	**a vernicle** an image of St Veronica

688 **biforn** before

689 **bretful of pardoun** full of pardons

690 **voys** voice

goot goat

693 **I trowe** I believe

697 **male** bag

pilwe-beer pillowcase

699 **gobet of the seil** a piece of the sail (as in the sail of St Peter's fishing boat)

700 **see** the sea

til Jhesu Crist him hente until Jesus Christ sent for him (to be an apostle)

701 **crois of latoun** a cross made of brass

703 **relikes** relics

706 **in monthes tweye** in two months

707 **feyned flaterye** false flattery

710 **a noble ecclesiaste** a noble churchman

712 **alderbest** best of all

offertorie an offering, a sung part of a church service

714 **wiste** knew

and well affile his tonge make his tongue smooth

716 **murierly** merrily

CONTEXT

The fallible churchman embroiled in sexual confusions – especially, in literature of the twentieth century, the bumbling Church of England vicar – has become a staple character in a certain type of **farcical** stage comedy. The Whitehall Farces, produced by Brian Rix in London's West End for many years, routinely featured a vicar overwhelmed by women.

THE INTRODUCTION TO *THE PARDONER'S TALE*

LINES 1–42

- The Host is sad and angry about the fate of the female heroine of the previous Tale – *The Physician's Tale* – and praises the Physician as a good fellow.
- He suggests that they all stop for a drink and ask the Pardoner to tell the next Tale.
- Some pilgrims demand a Tale with a good moral subject, and the Pardoner says he will think of one while he drinks.

CONTEXT

The Physician's Tale is a tragic though very flawed story set in classical times. In it a father kills his own daughter (apparently at her own request) so that she may die a virgin instead of being forcibly sexually conquered by a rapacious and evil judge. It is supposed to exemplify the moral that 'the wages of sin is death' (a quote from the Bible, Romans 6:23). In fact, the daughter is a victim of evil and the Tale is generally regarded as one of the weakest in *The Canterbury Tales*.

The 'Hooste' or Hoost (Chaucer uses both spellings in *The Pardoner's Tale*) swears that the poor girl in *The Physician's Tale* they have just heard was badly treated. He considers it a piteous Tale, but well told. He feels he needs a drink of 'moiste and corny' (29) ale after such a story. He calls on the Pardoner to tell the next Tale, and for him to make it a merry one. Some of the pilgrims demand a good **moral tale** with no coarseness. The Pardoner suggests they stop at the roadside inn they are passing where he will enjoy a drink while thinking of a suitable tale.

COMMENTARY

The first sixteen lines of this Introduction are the Host's response to the previous Tale. It is very much a linking section, one of many between Tales in the design of the overall work. Sometimes called, as in the Cambridge text, an 'Introduction', in other texts this section is entitled 'Words of the Host to the Physician and to the Pardoner'. These Introductions remind us that the band of pilgrims are listening to each Tale as they travel along the road, as well as providing an opportunity for **dialogue**, revealing more of the character of key figures as they interact with one another.

The Host speaks most of the Introduction in his customary informal, blunt way. He begins with 'Harrow!', a colloquial cry of distress and emotion, then utters a fairly mild curse 'by nailes and by blood!' (2). Chaucer observes that this swearing by the Host is habitual; he says he utters the curse 'as he were wood' (1) – as it was habit to do. His curse, referring to the nails that held Jesus to the cross and the blood he shed during the crucifixion, contains no real anger. It is just his manner of plain speaking. *The Physician's Tale* has moved him: he is sorry for the girl who died, who's 'beautee was hire deth' (11).

It is helpful to know a little about the character of the Host. He has volunteered to travel with the pilgrims, promising to keep everyone happy, be their guide to the route and be the arbiter between them in disputes. He does this elsewhere in the Tales, settling disagreements between the Miller and the Reeve, and the Friar and the Summoner, but in fact it is the Host's plain speaking that creates the dispute that concludes this Tale.

The Host is an amiable, likeable, and we assume, honest character. He is easily moved by the stories that are being told. He is in many ways the ideal publican: a little blunt and full of opinions, but generous in spirit and easy going. He is also a great literary device, used by Chaucer throughout *The Canterbury Tales* as a commentator. He links one story to the next via exchanges between himself and one or more of the pilgrims. In the structure of the cast of characters, the Host stands a little apart from the pilgrims, and he never tells a story himself.

The Host laments that the gifts of Fortune and Nature have been the cause of the death of many people (9–10). He is referring to a conventional belief of Chaucer's time that the gifts of Nature were held to be the natural qualities of a person's mind and body: the intelligence and beauty that they were born with. The gifts of Fortune were believed to be worldly rewards and achievements that determined a person's status in life. In Chaucer's day people placed more emphasis on luck and circumstance – on the random nature of fortune – and less on self-determination or planned and sustained personal effort to achieve success. For them, the gifts of Fortune were often randomly given. The Host says the girl in *The Physician's Tale* had both types of gifts.

CONTEXT

The Host is called Harry Bailey, landlord of the Tabard Inn from where the pilgrims have set out. He is offering a free dinner on their return to London for the best Tale told on the journey.

 CHECK THE BOOK

In *The General Prologue* the Host's 'manliness' is twice mentioned and is almost the first thing we learn about him. He is a 'semely' ('manly', 753) fellow who lacks nothing of 'manhede' ('manhood', 758). (Line numbers here refer to *The General Prologue to The Canterbury Tales*, Cambridge University Press, 2001.)

Looking at the *The Physician's Tale* and *The Pardoner's Tale* together in the sequence of stories, we can identify some implicit thematic connections. The idea of false justice and deception being the cause of unjust suffering for the morally good and the pious runs through both stories, though while the Physician merely tells his Tale with no input from himself beyond the telling, the Pardoner reveals his own morally corrupt personality in his.

The Host, being the sort of man he is, recovers his general good nature by line 17 and says they must pass on ('passe over') to another Tale. He praises the Physician for telling his Tale, concludes that he is a 'propre man' (23). He shows off his somewhat shaky knowledge of medical terms; he claims the Tale almost made him catch a 'cardynacle' (27) which some critics say means a heart attack, while others say it has no known modern meaning. He also confuses some names for medical equipment that he assumes the Physician will carry (19–21). He mentions 'galiones' but it is not clear exactly what this might mean. One suggestion is health giving drinks named after the Roman physician Galen (AD 129–99). By inventing this obscure term, Chaucer could be suggesting that the Host is making up what he does not know.

There is energy and good humour in every line of the Host's introduction. We can imagine him addressing the whole group, not one individual, and enjoying making himself the centre of attention. His repeated mild, though blasphemous, curses – 'by Seint Ronyan' (22) and 'By Corpus (Christ's) bones' (28) – seem high-spirited rather than real curses. Indeed, the free use of invocations of the saints seems catching, for the Pardoner also swears by 'Seint Ronyon' in his first line of speech (34). The Host's spelling indicates that it should be pronounced as three syllables; the Pardoner's spelling indicates just two. Said aloud, each pronunciation ensures that the line conforms to the ten syllable pattern of the verse. The pronunciation of many words in Middle English was different to our speech patterns today, and this can account for other lines which appear on first reading not to conform to the ten syllable measure. (See **Part Five: Further reading** for suggestions of audio versions of *The Pardoner's Tale* where you can hear how the text would have been spoken.)

> **CONTEXT**
>
> The Host and the Pardoner are both referring to St Ronan. The Catholic Church recognises twelve Irish saints called Ronan. Chaucer scholar J. De Weever in her book *The Chaucer Name Dictionary* (Routledge, 1988) suggests Chaucer probably had in mind the St Ronan who led a mission to pre-Christian Brittany, as he was the best known of these saints in Medieval England (page 316).

It is not clear in terms of the setting whether, after the Pardoner has thought up a story, everyone gets back on the road. They might in fact stay longer at the inn and gather round while the Pardoner, as he clearly wants to do, holds court and displays his skill in public speaking.

The Tale being told at the inn seems the more satisfying image. It is in the spirit of *The Canterbury Tales* that this particular group of pilgrims do not seem to seek to make their journey too arduous. They don't appear to be attempting to do penance by making a great effort in their pilgrimage: this is a pleasant trip as well as a religious undertaking to the shrine of England's then most revered unofficial patron saint. So perhaps it is best to imagine the Pardoner at the centre of a circle of pilgrims, sitting or standing about him, and enjoying a break from the road.

CHECK THE BOOK

St George is the official patron saint of England, but in the Middle Ages the (relatively) recently martyred Thomas à Becket was a hugely revered figure. The poet T. S. Eliot (1888–1965) wrote a play based on Becket's death, *Murder in the Cathedral*. He later rewrote the play as a film script.

GLOSSARY

3	**fals cherl** a false or cursed thief
4	**herte** heart
5	**thise juges** all such (false and evil) judges
6	**sely** innocent
9	**yiftes** gifts
14	**prow** benefit
17	**is no fors** let it pass
18	**so save thy gentil cors** a friendly remark, 'so save your gentle body' (in line 379 the word 'cors' is used specifically to mean corpse, so the meaning may be ambiguous)
19	**thine urinals and thy jurdones** chamberpots used to collect a patient's urine, the analysis of which was a part of medical practice in the fourteenth century
20	**ypocras** a drink of spiced wine, said to have mild medicinal properties
	galiones the Host is showing off his rather weak knowledge of medicine here, and this word has no meaning that we know about
21	**boyste** box
	letuarie medicine
24	**prelat** a bishop or other churchman of high office

continued

GLOSSARY

25	**speke in terme** speak using jargon, in this case medical
26	**thou doost myn herte to erme** you make my heart ache
27	**cardynacle** the meaning is not clear. It could mean heart attack, or Chaucer could be letting the Host make a deliberate mistake
28	**triacle** a remedy
30	**myrie** merry
32	**beel ami** Good friend, from the French, the language used in court for polite discourse
35	**alestake** the signpost outside an inn
38	**ribaudye** ribaldry
39	**leere** learn (some wit)
41	**I graunte ywis** I will do as you wish

THE PARDONER'S PROLOGUE

LINES 1–91

- The Pardoner says he always preaches on the same theme in church.
- He describes how he presents his (fake) holy relics.
- He tells the congregation what miraculous powers they have.

CONTEXT

The choice of the Pardoner's text from St Paul is doubly apt because Paul is the patron saint of preachers.

In this first section of his Prologue, the Pardoner describes how he sets about his business of getting people to buy pardons and holy relics from him when he preaches in church. His subject is always the same – *Radix malorum est cupiditas* – 'the love of money is the root of all evil'. This is a quote from the Bible, from St Paul's First Epistle to Timothy 6:10 where the line is actually *Radix omnium malorum est cupiditas*. Perhaps Chaucer did not bother to copy it exactly as it is such a well-known quote, or perhaps he is cunningly showing that the Pardoner is not as learned as he claims or thinks himself to be.

The Pardoner then recounts the claims he makes for his fake relics – bones and rags sealed in bottles that he lets the congregation believe are the bodily relics of holy men or objects formerly associated with them. He describes how he has a sheep's shoulder bone in a case that he claims will, if immersed in a well, cure sick animals that drink there. He does not conceal from the pilgrims that all this is deception and trickery designed to help him make money – in fact he is clearly proud of his ability to deceive. The pilgrims, expecting an introduction to a **moral tale**, are getting a startling and unashamed confession of fraud.

COMMENTARY

From the first moment it is clear that the Pardoner is no humble preacher, full of piety and religious belief. There is pride in the way he describes his preaching style – he takes pains to maintain a haughty – 'hauteyn' (44) – style of speech and he is proud of his voice that rings out as 'gooth [as the sound of] a belle' (45). He has learnt his **sermon** by heart: 'For I kan al by rote that I telle' (46) and we sense that his words are no more than a skilful salesman's patter, used to persuade his customers to buy his wares. At the beginning of his Prologue he self-importantly takes the stage as he prepares to let his travelling companions into the tricks of his trade.

The Pardoner lays out in a clear order his approach to his work. He tells a congregation where he comes from, 'whennes that I come' (49). Then he shows them his various letters of authority, 'bulles' (50), and 'oure lige lordes seel' (52), which is a letter or licence displaying a bishop's seal. Official church documents would have been written in Latin which only scholars and other churchmen could understand, so the Pardoner could in fact be presenting a simple country congregation with almost any official-looking document. Finally before he begins showing his wares, he speaks a 'fewe' words of Latin (58). The 'fewe' suggests this is further showmanship and that any words in Latin will do. The Pardoner's tone throughout this passage is businesslike, describing his practical approach to preaching. There is no hint that what he does is driven by genuine piety: equally, he does not yet confess that he has absolutely no belief in what he says or does. (This is not revealed until lines 141–2, 'Thus kan I preche again that same vice/ Which that I use, and that is avarice'). Here the Pardoner describes what he does in a theatrical way, but doesn't dare to say anything that might

QUESTION Is the Pardoner a confident character who believes the pilgrims will endorse what he confesses, or is he so self-obsessed that he doesn't see the likely effect his words may have on the others?

contradict the law of the Church. The penalty for exposing the Church's hypocrisy would be jail, or worse.

Religion and money were closely connected in Chaucer's time, and selling pardons and holy relics was an important source of income for the Catholic Church. The Church was suffering what would be called a 'cash flow crisis' today. It owned great buildings and vast tracts of productive farmland, but in fact earned very little from these assets. The Vatican (the spiritual and administrative heart of the Church in Rome, overseen by the Pope, its supreme leader) decided to create pardoners as a way of raising additional funds. Pardoners were lay people (not ordained priests) who could collect holy relics and claim miraculous, usually curative, properties for them. Bits of bone supposed to have come from the skeleton of a long-dead saint and pickled in bottles, scraps of rag claimed to be cut from their clothing and other rather unsavoury scraps were the usual items offered. Most relics were in fact made by pardoners or other tricksters.

Pardoners could travel from church to church within a certain area, and sell these relics to people who could pay. For those with less money, the pardoner could issue 'pardons'. These were written or verbal agreements that, in return for a few coins, allowed the purchaser to be let off certain fast days or be absolved from minor sins. In return for acting as 'travelling salesmen' for these pardons and relics, pardoners could keep a percentage of the money they took from congregations, and give the rest to the Church.

The system soon collapsed into corruption. Pardoners often kept more than was agreed or just kept all the money that people gave them. They would concoct new relics to sell. Even in such deeply religious times, many people secretly thought pardoners were corrupt peddlers of rubbish. Chaucer's readers would have enjoyed seeing a popularly distrusted figure they would recognise, maybe even have met in a church, willingly expose himself as a fraud. Perhaps we should imagine the less pious of the pilgrims laughing along with the Pardoner as he gleefully explains his deceptions, while the more religious or morally upright shudder.

CONTEXT

In Chaucer's day there existed what were believed to be genuine and therefore highly-prized relics of famous saints. These would have been beyond the reach of any pardoner. Many of these relics survive today – most commonly those claiming to be a bone from a saint's body. It is not impossible for several different churches to have what purports to be the same bone from the same saint on display.

Despite the commonly-held view that pardoners were frequently dishonest, most people were intensely religious, and most believed in supernatural powers and in miracles. A convincing pardoner could sell a lot of relics and pardons, and make enough money to live well. Communications between one part of the country and another were almost non-existent, for poor people especially, so a pardoner could hope to get away with this deception for years if he was lucky, and even evade investigation from the Church. The situation eventually prompted Pope Boniface IX to issue a letter in 1390, which exposed exactly the sort of corruption practised by the Pardoner.

This section of *The Pardoner's Prologue* is a catalogue of descriptions of the relics he carries and the lies he tells about them. He describes the false claims he makes for one of his relics, a sheep's bone in a brass case. It isn't clear if he tells congregations that it is an animal bone that he could have picked up anywhere on his travels, or if he lets them believe that its supposed curative powers come from the fact that it is something more rare and holy – a bone from the skeleton of a holy man perhaps. Given the Pardoner's attitude, it is safe to assume he lets them think the latter. To the pilgrims, he describes this relic as the bone of a 'hooly Jewes sheep' (65), which critics variously suggest is a mildly anti-Semitic joke or an attempt at a vague reference to an unspecified Old Testament figure.

The Pardoner tells congregations that if they put this holy bone in a well the water will acquire the power to cure sick animals which drink there or have their tongues washed in it. In a society based on farming the health of livestock was of huge importance. A crueller element is therefore added to the tricks the Pardoner plays – his well-practised deception might well have the effect of encouraging poor farmers to give him hard-earned money for a relic that will, in fact, do nothing to avert the tragedy of dying animals.

As if warming to his theme, or perhaps enjoying a sense of getting the weight of his habitual deceptions off his chest, the Pardoner gives the pilgrims two more examples of the extravagant and utterly false claims that he makes for his worthless relics. He says that the same bone he has already described as having healing qualities can

> **CONTEXT**
>
> In his letter Pope Boniface referred to pardoners who falsely claimed to have come directly from Rome, instructed to conduct 'a mission to receive money for the Roman church', and who went 'about the country under these pretexts', just as Chaucer's Pardoner claims in *The General Prologue*.

CONTEXT

The Catholic Church in the Middle Ages was rich in relics that supposedly had miraculous powers. The power to cure illnesses and to make women fertile were common claims.

also aid a woman to prevent jealousy in her husband. Placed into water again, this time he claims that the bone will create a miraculous fluid that she can use to make her husband's soup, 'potage' (82). Suddenly, he will never more mistrust his wife, even if she takes two or three priests for lovers – 'Al had she taken prestes two or thre' (85).

Suggesting that a 'holy' relic has the morally dubious quality of blinding someone to sin and a personal injustice is a remarkable claim to make to a congregation in a church. Furthermore, the fact that he singles out priests for the woman's lovers gives an extra edge to his duplicity. The Pardoner seems to be heaping scorn on both moral principles and the Church, and demonstrating personal contempt for both. The pilgrims who exorted him (in the Introduction to the Tale) to avoid ribald or bawdy subject matter must now be thinking they are being offered something far more offensive: a personal confession of moral and spiritual corruption.

It would add so much to our understanding of how the pilgrims operated as a group of characters through the Tales if we could 'see' how they reacted at key moments to stories as they unfolded. This would be especially interesting in the case of *The Pardoner's Tale* which involves such a large element of what would have been to them shocking confessions. Chaucer however limits their comments on Tales to introductions and conclusions. Chaucer's method is for each speaker to hold the stage alone while telling their Tale: he is not writing a work where characters constantly interact through **dialogue**, as they might in a play. Scripted drama, as we understand the **genre**, had not been invented in Chaucer's time. We can only guess at how Chaucer wanted us to imagine how different characters in the group of pilgrims would be reacting to the growing venom and bitterness expressed by the Pardoner in his Prologue. Some might be shocked by his singling out churchmen for their immoral sexual behaviour, others might be laughing. Many people believed that all wives would be unfaithful given a chance and that priests, men not wise in the ways of the world, would break the very rules they preached. Seen through any more easy-going pilgrims' eyes, the Pardoner is not so much venomous as providing a traditional, almost knock-about comic example of life as it is really lived.

However, we can imagine that by now, at the end of a fairly remarkable list of obviously false claims, the other pilgrims are 'all ears', intently listening to what amounts to an amazing confession of abusing people's religious faith. In his Introduction, the Pardoner confesses that he needs a drink while he thinks of a suitably moral story to tell: it is possible that the pilgrims are now wondering whether he has drunk too much and will reveal things he wouldn't admit to if he was sober. They would certainly be considering what has happened to the promised moral theme, despite the supposedly religious subject matter.

CHECK THE BOOK

The other great literary work to survive from Chaucer's time is *Piers Plowman*, a long poem (it survives in three versions from 2,500 to 7,500 lines in length) attributed to William Langland. It contains discussions on farm labour and elements of the lives of agricultural labourers.

GLOSSARY

43	**Lordinges** ladies and gentlemen
46	**I kan al by rote** I can recite word for word from memory
50	**bulles** a Papal Bull is a document signed by the Pope. The lead seal that he uses to stamp his authority on them is called in Latin a 'bulla', hence the name. They are still issued
51	**lige lordes** liege lords, as in lords to whom someone owes allegiance, in this case who grant the Pardoner's authority and to whom he supposedly reports
	patente a letter of approval, in this case from the Church to the Pardoner for him to show to people who doubt his authority
54	**Me to destourbe** to prevent me (from preaching)
59	**saffron with my predicacioun** to give flavour and colour to my preaching. Saffron is a natural cooking ingredient
60	**stire hem to devocioun** stir them to devotion
61	**cristal stones** bottles (containing pickled relics)
62	**cloutes** rags
63	**as wenen they echoon** as everyone understands
64	**Thanne have I in latoun a sholder-boon** latoun is a form of brass, presumably here meaning some sort of metal case, in which the Pardoner keeps a bone

continued

GLOSSARY

66	**taak of my wordes keep** listen to what I say
67	**wassh** washed
69	**ystonge** stung
71	**hool anon** soon healed
72	**pokkes** pox
74	**eek** also
76	**Wol every wyke** will every week
80	**heeleth jalousie** heals jealousy
82	**potage** a thin soup
85	**he the soothe of hir defaute wiste** if he knew the truth of her (his wife's) faults
87	**miteyn** a mitten, used by peasants for hand-sowing seeds
90	**So that he offer pens, or elles groats** as long as he offers pennies or groats. A groat was a coin worth four pennies, quite a lot for a poor peasant farmer in the 1390s

For further analysis of this section of the Prologue, see **Extended commentaries Text 1**.

LINES 92–136

- The Pardoner makes further false claims for his holy relics.

- He quotes the special trick he has for getting congregations to purchase pardons.

- He makes it clear that the money he extracts he keeps for himself.

- He shows the depths of his distain for the people he cheats. He has no care for what happens to their souls and silences any objections they make.

QUESTION

The Pardoner appears to relish sharing the way he deceives people and how he spends the money he tricks out of them. Can you identify any comic aspects in his character?

The Pardoner continues to describe the claims he makes for the relics he sells. He explains his trick to make people more willing to come forward to purchase pardons: he suggests that reluctance to buy them implies a degree of sinfulness beyond the help of such pardons. He says that he keeps for himself the money he so successfully extracts from people to fund his own living. He reveals the disdain he has for those he cheats, and describes how he prevents anyone he suspects might try to speak out against him or any other pardoners from doing so. The tone of this section grows increasingly dark as the Pardoner reveals more and more of his deceitful ways and unpleasant nature.

COMMENTARY

Whether you read the end of the previous section of *The Pardoner's Prologue* as ribald mockery or as a bitter declamation, it is in these next forty-four lines that the Pardoner shows the darker depths of his tricky and the utter disdain he has for the people he cheats.

The Pardoner has been speaking within inverted commas since line 66: he is quoting to the pilgrims the form of words he uses when addressing congregations. He now (91) reaches the hook in his trick, the final part of his extended quote, up to line 102. He tells those he is preaching to that he cannot pardon anyone who has committed truly horrible sins: 'that hath doon sinne horrible' (93). He imagines there may be people present who dare not for shame come forward to be 'yshriven' (94), forgiven. Again he singles out women who have been unfaithful to their husbands, who have made them 'cokewold' (96), cuckolds – that is, husbands whose wives are adulterous with other men. The Pardoner is again appealing to the popular notion of the time that women, especially attractive or sexually active ones, were naturally morally frail creatures who could not help but commit adultery whenever the chance arose.

The Pardoner says that only those sinners who feel able to acquit themselves of blame can benefit from his pardons, and that they should therefore come forward to purchase the relics and pardons. Of course, the idea is that everyone comes forward, fearing that if they remain sitting in their pews then people will think they are guilty of the sort of gross sins the Pardoner maintains he does not have the authority to forgive. Creating this dilemma for the congregation for his own subsequent gain, is the central point of his whole process of deception. He plays on both their personal insecurities and their social reputations.

> **CONTEXT**
>
> 'Cuckold' was a common term of insult in medieval and later England. It has a long history of references and **imagery** in literature. Cuckolds were also often portrayed as having or being made to wear stag's antlers. This refers to Actaeon, who in Greek mythology surprised the Goddess Diana bathing naked and was turned by her into a stag.

After the Pardoner has quoted from his sermon the speech marks are closed (102) and he reverts to talking directly and specifically to his fellow pilgrims. It is from here on that the tone of what the Pardoner says darkens, and his confession becomes something more personal and unlike any other Tale in the whole collection. No other character reveals himself so fully and deliberately. No other pilgrim puts themselves such a morally bad light.

Spiritual corruption and the abuse of Church power do feature in other Tales, however. The Friar tells a Tale about a dishonest summoner and the Summoner responds by telling a bawdy and defamatory story abut a friar. Both Tales involve morally and materially corrupt Church figures, but only as characters within Tales. The Pardoner speaks about himself and much of his story is a true account of his life. His confession makes his Tale unique in the collection. He never once asks the pilgrims what they think of what they are learning about him. It is as if he either doesn't care, or is supremely confident that they will approve of him. That is a great leap of faith: to confess habitual abuse of people's religious beliefs to a group of pilgrims and expect them not to object.

The Pardoner tells the pilgrims that by this 'gaude' (103) or trick he has made a living of a hundred marks every year since he became a pardoner. He is clearly proud of this record, and we may suggest that he is adding the sin of pride to the many others he commits.

The Pardoner describes how he stands 'lyk a clerk in my pulpet' (105) – 'like a priest or cleric in my pulpit'. He says that he preaches 'an hundred false japes moore' (108). 'Japes' usually means jokes but here it means false stories. He is expressly forbidden by church rules to act like a priest, and the use of 'my' to describe the pulpit, the platform from which the priest should command the church, reveals much about the Pardoner's sense of self-importance. He describes the 'lewed' (106) people in the congregation sitting down. 'Lewed' means both lay, as in not churchmen or women, and ignorant. It is their ignorance and specifically their illiteracy (which makes them easier to deceive) that he is identifying here. This whole section, up to line 137, is coloured by the Pardoner's sense of self-importance and his contempt for others.

CHECK THE FILM

The Name of the Rose, a film version of the novel of the same name by Umberto Eco, is set in a medieval monastery where the monks enjoy a good life while the lay population outside its walls struggle in poverty.

CONTEXT

A mark was worth (in pre-decimal currency units) thirteen shillings and four pence, two-thirds of one pound. In Chaucer's time a hundred marks was a huge yearly income.

From lines 110 to 120 the Pardoner speaks with relish about his skill at preaching and his contempt for the people who come to hear him, and for the lies he tells them. He delights in his misdeeds. He ends this section with a striking rhyming couplet, saying that once they have been buried – 'beried' – he doesn't care what happens to their souls: for all he cares they could have gone blackberrying – 'goon a-blakeberied' (119–20) – a harmless country pastime. It is at once a trivial and a spiteful remark, and one that would shock the more religious pilgrims for whom belief in and concern for an afterlife was an ever-present element of their faith.

The Pardoner also describes how he stretches his neck like a bird and studies the people (109–11). From the unflattering physical description we have of the Pardoner in *The General Prologue*, this must be a very unattractive sight, not at all like the dove on a roof that he sees it as. Despite its deliberate inaccuracy, revealing the Pardoner's self-delusion, this is a good example of the vivid visual **imagery** that the Pardoner employs throughout his Tale. He is speaking aloud to the pilgrims (and to his imaginary congregation), and Chaucer knew that many of his contemporaries would have had *The Canterbury Tales* read aloud to them. Chaucer understood the **rhetorical** power in giving them 'pictures in words' to imagine.

> **CONTEXT**
>
> In Christian art, the dove symbolises the Holy Ghost. The Pardoner is abusing this powerful symbolism by choosing to describe himself as a dove when he is at his most venomous.

The Pardoner seems to be sailing close to a dangerous condemnation of the Church at times. It may be fair enough to wring some humour out of the idea that priests were as fallible as the rest of us when it comes to being tempted by other men's wives. However, when the Pardoner says that many a 'predicacioun' or **sermon** (121) comes from evil intention, or from hypocritical flattery to gain advancement or promotion (123–4), he is widening his criticism potentially to include all priests who preach sermons. This degree of seemingly genuine anger towards the Church does not occur in any other of *The Canterbury Tales*. Other attacks on the Church are usually tempered with comedy.

Vocabulary and **imagery** are powerfully focused to reveal a darker mood. The Pardoner will 'stinge' opponents with his 'smerte' (sharp) tongue (127). He will 'spitte I out my venym' (135). These reptilian images suggest that the Pardoner, a man who appears to like his own appearance – he sees it as fashionable, not freakish as Chaucer obviously does in *The General Prologue* – is revealing another, darker self-image. He is showing, somewhat perversely perhaps, that he is a man not to be meddled with. The image of a venomous snake would recall for many of Chaucer's audience the serpent in the Garden of Eden, Eve's tempter and the Devil's agent.

His venom is reserved for anyone in the congregation who dares criticise his 'bretheren' (130), by which he means other pardoners. This is the first and only time that we hear him refer to others who follow his profession, and the assumption contained in the idea of brethren is that they also work for their own ends as he does. The Pardoner might seem quite a lonely figure – travelling around the country alone and probably not wanting to keep close to other people given what he is doing – but here we glimpse that perhaps he is part of a band of pardoners who work alone but feel part of a group. The Pardoner says he enjoys spending what he tricks out of congregations on good living. There is no evidence to suggest that he is a miser or a hoarder so we might think of him as the life and soul of celebrations in ale houses, so long as he keeps this side of his character hidden from the public gaze.

We might also imagine this most dark and aggressive section in the Prologue so far contains a warning to the pilgrims. The Pardoner may suspect that some of them might react with anger or outrage to his confession, so he casually describes how he is an enemy to be reckoned with by anyone in a congregation who might try some similar criticism. If any of the pilgrims were tempted to challenge him, then this passage might ensure they remained silent. There is a sinister though unspecified threat to back this up in lines 131–3 where the Pardoner says that anyone he discovers to have 'trespased to my bretheren or to me' will not be named but they will 'wel knowe' they are discovered by 'signes, and by othere circumstances'.

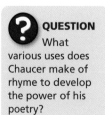

QUESTION What various uses does Chaucer make of rhyme to develop the power of his poetry?

A simple, striking rhyme, 'hewe/…trewe' (136–7) neatly concludes this section of the Pardoner's long and by now dark and unsettling confession. What follows, however, is only a change of direction, not a lightening of tone or subject.

GLOSSARY

98	**offren** to offer
101	**assoille** absolve
	auctoritee authority
106	**doun yset** set down
109	**Thanne peyne I me** then I take pains
110	**bekke** to nod the head
112	**goon so yerne** to walk or go busily
116	**yeven hir pens** given his pennies
118	**correccioun** correction
119	**I rekke nevere** I never care
121	**For certes** for certainly
123	**plesance of folk and flaterye** to give pleasure and to flatter people
124	**avaunched by ypocrisye** to gain advancement by being hypocritical
125	**veyne glorie** false pride
128	**nat asterte** not avoid
130	**Hath trespased** have trespassed or crossed in the sense of contradicted or made angry
134	**Thus quyte I folk that doon us displesances** 'Thus I make those who have displeased me keep quiet'
135	**under hewe** under the colour or pretence of
136	**semen** seeming

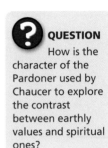

QUESTION
How is the character of the Pardoner used by Chaucer to explore the contrast between earthly values and spiritual ones?

LINES 137–76

- The Pardoner explains that the subject of his **sermon** is always the sin of avarice.
- He describes in graphic terms his love of money and repeats that he preaches purely for personal gain.
- He asks the pilgrims if they are ready for a tale, and assures them that he is a good storyteller.

Without actually saying that he does not believe in God or the rules of the Church, the Pardoner says that nothing he does is for any spiritual or charitable purpose, but always and only for his own material gain. It is a forceful, almost proud, declaration of committing the sin of avarice. As a confession, it is full of the sin of pride for the actions being confessed. The Pardoner repeats with more emphasis his disdain for the poor people he cheats in cruelly vivid images, and claims to use the money he gains to enjoy a good life of wine and women. Then he quickly concludes his description of his life and reminds the pilgrims that he has a tale to tell them.

COMMENTARY

The Pardoner begins this final section of his Prologue by revealing clearly and simply his intentions as a preacher and a granter of pardons. The idea of saying, in line 137, and later in line 148, what one intends to talk about is a typical device of medieval poetry, and of much storytelling within oral traditions. Most people would be listening, just like the pilgrims, to the story, not reading the text. They could not go back and re-read, so structural devices like these would help them assimilate what is being read or told to them.

The Pardoner declares 'I preche of no thing but for coveitise' (138). He repeats the same line at 147, the only example of such exact repetition in the Tale. Chaucer wants to make sure his audience are clear on this key point about the Pardoner: his preaching is driven purely by his own covetousness. The Pardoner re-asserts that his theme is always based on the same text *Radix malorum est cupiditas*

CONTEXT

Travelling minstrels who collected and sang **ballads** were an important feature of popular culture in medieval England. Their ballad and story repertoires contained both new works designed to convey news of events, and variations of well-known traditional stories. It is possible that the basic tale on which Chaucer based *The Pardoner's Tale* was part of this folk repertoire.

– 'the love of money is the root of all evil'. Just in case any of the pilgrims are still in doubt about his intentions, the Pardoner states clearly between the repeated lines (141–2) that he is guilty of the 'vice' that he preaches against.

Chaucer is writing throughout *The Canterbury Tales* in a relatively simple **rhyming couplet** verse pattern. This could become repetitive, but it is the range of **voices** he creates, and the individual vividness of each of them, that makes the whole work so varied and dynamic. The Pardoner's is one of the most striking. It is without any of the humour and humanity of the other pilgrims. His confession of his deceits is not warmed with humour or softened by self-deprecation. Yet his confidence and skill as a public speaker or preacher comes through, and though he may not persuade the pilgrims to approve of his actions, he does engage and entertain them with his range of references, his use of **imagery**, his pace of moving through his subject matter and with the general energy of his speaking. All these elements are to be found in this final section of *The Pardoner's Prologue*.

He makes a surprising claim for his effectiveness as a preacher, over and above his skill in tricking congregations out of their money. He says that though he is sinful, he can 'maken oother folk to twynne/ from avarice' (144–5), he can make others 'depart' from committing the sin of avarice. Furthermore, he says he can make them repent. He is implicitly claiming that his sermons do perform spiritual good: by taking him at face value congregations are saved from further sinning and repent the sins they have already committed. It could also be that they will have less opportunity to sin having given what little money they had to the preacher for the pardons.

We may see in this a glimmer of a positive outcome from the Pardoner's corrupt practices. Yet the Pardoner does not allow a moment of possible justification for himself to stand, because he immediately says that if these positive outcomes occur that is not his principle intention. He does not pursue this issue further, for at line 148 he says simply 'Of this mateere it oghte ynogh suffise' – that ought to be enough on this subject. This is another structural device for an audience imagined to be listening to the Prologue, telling them to put this matter aside and prepare for a new direction in the story.

 CHECK THE BOOK
Ambrose Bierce (1842–1913) was an American journalist who wrote one famous book, the satirical *Devil's Dictionary*, a collection of a thousand humorous definitions of words. He expanded this into *The Enlarged Devil's Dictionary* (Penguin, 1989) which includes many religious and theological definitions that would no doubt amuse the Pardoner.

The Pardoner now returns to the idea of conveying to the pilgrims his rhetorical skills as a preacher. Whereas previously (66–102) he quoted the actual words he might speak to a congregation, now he describes in general terms how he preaches. He uses many 'ensamples' (149). This is a technical term describing stories told to illustrate a general truth, an extremely common device in medieval sermons.

The Pardoner does not give examples of the stories he tells, because the pace and tone of the Prologue is hurrying on into a further confession. The tone becomes highly personal and charged. We can imagine the Pardoner using the devices of surprise and appeal in his delivery to the pilgrims gathered round. He asks the rhetorical question – 'why, as long as I can preach so successfully, should I then choose to live in poverty?' (153–5). He is not, of course, asking the pilgrims actually to answer this, but he is encouraging them to think how they would act in his situation. He concludes this veiled appeal for their understanding with the heartfelt 'Nay, nay, I thoght it nevere (I never think it) trewely!' (156).

QUESTION
Deception is a constant theme in *The Pardoner's Tale*. How does Chaucer explore this theme in different ways?

Throughout his Prologue, the Pardoner swaps from one idea to another, often destroying the effect he might have created in his listeners. His change of subject now is an example of this. One or two of the less morally upright pilgrims might be swayed by his rhetoric, but the Pardoner goes on to describe graphically and viciously the depths of his greed and his disregard for the harm he causes. Chaucer leaves us to decide why the Pardoner is so graphic in his confession. Does the Pardoner feel so confident of the respect the pilgrims hold him in, because of his work, that they will tolerate what he says? Or does he believe he is telling them such a good tale about his deceptions that he wants to embellish it for dramatic effect? Or is this in fact something closer to a 'true confession', in which the Pardoner exposes the depths of his misdeeds so as to tell the absolute truth for once?

He says he will never beg while he can preach for his own ends. Neither will he 'make baskettes' (159) a reference to St Paul the Hermit, who made baskets for a living. The Pardoner compares his intentions with those of a figure who was both holy and an honest worker. He says that he will not labour with his hands (158). He concludes this powerfully confessional passage by saying that he will 'noon of the apostles countrefete' (161) – he will not seek to imitate the apostles who were genuinely holy figures.

The Pardoner compares the things he buys with his 'ill gotten gains' with the image of the poorest widow in a village who gives him money for a worthless pardon even though her children might then starve (164–5). In the line after this dreadful image he says that he 'will have' – as if it is his right – wine, 'licour of the vine' (167), and a wench in every town. Given his strange appearance and the physical signs noted in his description in *The General Prologue*, which leads Chaucer to suggest he might be a eunuch, this aspect of the Pardoner's idea of a good life might surprise us, and perhaps affirms the boastful – and possibly self-deluded – nature of his speech.

CHECK THE BOOK

For detailed historical background on the harsh realities of life in England in the Middle Ages, read *Medieval England 1000–1500: A Reader*, Emilie Amt (Editor) (Broadview Press, 2000). It contains essays on the Great Famine, the Black Death and the Peasants' Revolt.

There is a final line to assist the listener at the end of this graphic and grim section. The Pardoner asks (168) the company to listen to his conclusion. He is now ready to tell his Tale. He has drunk his ale – an image of sated appetite that contrasts to his disregard for the widow and children starving – and he admits that though he is a 'vicious' man (174) he can tell a good moral story. He can speak passionately for ideals he does not personally hold. This is a clear example of the theme of deception that runs through his Prologue and Tale, of things not being as they appear. It is given a complex twist here, for the Pardoner is definitely not the man he appears to be to the congregations he tricks, yet here he is apparently revealing his true nature to the pilgrims. He is about to tell them the sort of story he usually preaches for gain, and he asks them to hold their peace.

Again it would be so revealing here if Chaucer had indicated by interjections from other characters their emotional responses to what they are being told. Is 'Now hoold youre pees' (176) just a rhetorical flourish to a group of silent, rapt pilgrims? Or are we to imagine murmurs of dissent caused by the unpleasant images of the Pardoner's greed that have preceded this final section? Are they rebelling against this smug, grasping hypocrite suddenly revealed in their midst? Or are they stunned into silence by the honesty of the Pardoner's confession? Are they even laughing at his villainy? Or are they just all ears for a Tale from a professional storyteller for which this lengthy Prologue has been operating as a build up? These questions are as rhetorical as those the Pardoner poses to the pilgrims – and like them require no absolute answer.

GLOSSARY

144	**twynne**	to depart from or leave behind
146	**entente**	intention
150	**agoon**	ago
152	**things kan they well reporte and hold**	things they can learn and remember
153	**trowe ye**	do you think
154	**teche**	teach
157	**sondry landes**	sundry lands, different places
161	**countrefete**	imitate
162	**wolle**	wool
	whete	wheat, as in food
176	**pees**	peace

THE PARDONER'S TALE

LINES 177–98

- The Pardoner introduces the Flemish tavern where his Tale will begin, in which is a 'compaignye', who lead riotous lives of excess and sin.
- The Pardoner specifically identifies their sin of drunkenness.

This is a short and simple passage in which the Pardoner introduces and briefly describes a group of riotous young men, before he moves into a 'demonstration' **sermon** on the sins these men habitually commit. These sins include excessive eating and drinking, gambling and sexual temptation and indulgence, but it is drinking that receives the most attention.

This short introductory section of the Tale requires a separate commentary to explore a few key points. Much of this passage employs a universal perspective in the way the Pardoner reviews the sins the men commit. He speaks of sins rather than their specific sinful habits. This deliberate universalising is linked to the Pardoner's decision to set the Tale in a foreign country: one he could be fairly

? QUESTION

Chaucer does not make clear whether the 'company' of young folk he introduces is a crowd that *includes* the three young men who will be the main characters of his Tale, or whether he is referring to them alone. The Pardoner does not specifically identify them as 'thise riotoures thre' until line 375 where he returns to the Tale after his sermon. Is this ambiguity deliberate, do you think?

sure none in the congregations he preaches to will have visited. (Chaucer himself did visit Flanders, in 1377, on unspecified state business; see **Historical background**.) The location and the sense of universal sinfulness creates a detached, almost fairytale, atmosphere for the Tale. The use of 'whilom' in the opening line (177) adds to this almost mythic mood: in medieval poetry and storytelling, 'whilom' approximated to 'once upon a time', a declaration that this was not necessarily a true telling of events but more an archetypal tale. The Pardoner wants his listeners (congregations and the pilgrims) to infer that similar sins are practised in their own society, but he wants to avoid potential accusations of direct social criticism. Imagine how much more personally felt the Tale might be by some of the pilgrims (the Host especially) if the Pardoner set it in a London or Kentish tavern. Its reception could have been very different and its clear moral message confused.

The use of the word 'whilom' also adds another dimension – the Pardoner is implying that this is not a tale of his own invention. The fact that it is set in another country (at a time when most ordinary people rarely moved out of their own localities) further adds to the sense that this is a story that has been handed on and passed down. This device is used to introduce several other Tales. Audiences in Chaucer's day placed much less emphasis on artistic originality than we do now. Often a familiar story well told, with convincing new details and small, engaging additions, was preferred to a new story badly constructed.

The sins of the company are all based upon riotous living. The Pardoner does not accuse them of other sins, for example being cheats or deceivers. They 'riot', play at dice, eat and drink to excess; and presumably, given the mention of 'tombesteres' (191) or dancing girls and of 'baudes' (193) or pimps, they are also guilty of sexual lust. The Pardoner also mentions confectioners, providers of luxury sweet foods, in this extensive and extravagant list of temptations provided by the 'verray develes officeres' (194). These are the dancing girls who 'kindle and blowe the fyr of lecherye' (195). Hell and the Devil are often invoked in images of heat and flames, and people in the grip of erotic desire are often described as inflamed. This section focuses more on sexual sin and the 'temptations of the flesh' than any other part of the Tale. In keeping

CONTEXT

A detached, non-naturalistic and sometimes vaguely specified setting is typical of much literature in the **gothic** as well as folk tradition. Bram Stoker set much of the action of his gothic novel *Dracula* (1897) in the Carpathian Mountains, which few of his contemporary readers would have ever visited or even been able to locate on an atlas.

CONTEXT

Feminist critics have written at great length about many of *The Canterbury Tales.* The role of women in the medieval conception of marriage as revealed in *The Miller's Tale* and *The Wife of Bath's Tale* is a subject that has been much reviewed, as has the moral predicament and mortal fate of Virginia in *The Physician's Tale.*

CHECK THE BOOK

The idea of sinful living based on hard drinking, gambling and lechery within a tavern is an enduring image in English literature. Two hundred years after Chaucer, Shakespeare created the Boar's Head Tavern in his great history plays *Henry IV Parts 1* and *2.* Frequented by prostitutes and drunken knights, it is an English version of the Pardoner's unruly Flanders tavern.

with medieval gender attitudes, though the men are to be presented as habitual sinners, women (dancing girls) are presented as not merely temptresses, but as actively prompting the Devil's work through their erotic behaviour.

The Pardoner creates a world of symbolic over-indulgence and types of excessive sinner to suit the moral purpose of the story. He provides a full list of the sins that attend immoderate good living such as these three men seek to indulge in. The pilgrims must have enjoyed hearing such a carnival of temptations of the flesh laid out before them. Carnival atmosphere pervades many of the other Tales, and is generally absent from this much darker one. A short interlude in which to imagine a tavern crammed with sinfulness must have been welcome. It is of course intended to be a shocking place, a palace of temptations, but it could be argued that people have always been thrilled by things they know are not good for them.

The Pardoner makes particular reference to swearing and the use of oaths which blaspheme against the name of Christ. Many common oaths in Chaucer's time referred to Christ's body and the wounds it received during the crucifixion. 'God's blood' and 'God's wounds' were commonly uttered. The Host automatically and without any real venom curses 'by nails and by blood' at the very start of the Introduction, a reference to the crucifixion. When in lines 188–9 the Pardoner talks of them **metaphorically** tearing apart, 'totere', or torturing Christ's body again in their curses, he says that it was as if the three sinful men did not believe that the Jews had hurt him enough. This remark is strongly anti-Semitic, but such an attitude was common and accepted in Chaucer's England.

GLOSSARY

177	**Flaundres** Flanders
178	**haunteden folye** fully gave themselves up to
179	**hasard** gambling
	stywes stews, brothels
180	**harpes, lutes, and giternes** stringed instruments used to play music for dances

181	pleyen at dees play at dice
183	they doon the devel sacrifise they make worshipful sacrifice to the devil
185	superfluitee abhominable awful excess
186	othes oaths
188	totere torture
189	rente him noght ynough had not wounded him (Jesus) enough
190	otheres sinne lough laughed at other sins
191	tombesteres dancing girls
192	Fetys graceful
	smale small, as in graceful and slim
	frutesteres fruit sellers
193	baudes pimps, procurers of prostitutes
	wafereres sellers of sweets and chocolates
195	fyr fire

CHECK THE POEM

Philip Larkin's poem 'The Card Players' (from *High Windows*, Faber, 1974) is set in a tavern similar to the one the Pardoner wants his listeners to imagine. Larkin creates a world of grotesque characters (Jan van Hogspeuw, Dirk Dogstoerd) engaging in the sort of crude behaviour the Pardoner imagines. But Larkin's last line with its two exclamation marks suggests something to celebrate in their crude but timeless indulgence, 'Rain, wind and fire! The secret, bestial peace!'

LINES 199–262

- The Pardoner condemns the sin of drunkenness.

- He employs biblical and classical references to condemn gluttony.

- He paints an earthy and vivid picture of the physical effects of excessive eating.

- He emphasises the idea that to consume to excess is to waste and dishonour God's gifts.

The Pardoner now gives the pilgrims a detailed and extended sample of his skill as a preacher. He uses biblical and classical allusions to broaden his attack against the sins of drunkenness and gluttony, and he supports his sermonising by reference to a wide range of similar thought and opinion. He describes the evils of drunkenness first, and then moves on to gluttony. In both cases, he balances apparently learned references to biblical and historical figures who drank or ate to excess with very earthy and vivid pictures of the physical effects of over-indulgence.

COMMENTARY

By moving through various sins, the Pardoner demonstrates his understanding of the medieval idea that to commit one sin leads the way to committing others. The reverse of sin – goodness or grace – was seen as a quality that must not be tarnished by any misdeeds. Once a sin had been committed, the way was open for all other sins to be committed. People believed that God and the Devil were locked in an on-going battle, a battle in which God fought to defend and gather to him the good and holy, while the Devil tried to tempt people into sin to gather them to him, to hell and damnation. Today, we may regard doing something bad as a lapse of personal moral behaviour, the breaking of a human code that we choose to try to live by. But for Chaucer's pilgrims committing a sin was a more universal matter. Once they had sinned they were drawn into the great battle between good and evil. For them, one of the most horrifying things about the three sinners would be that they apparently feel no need to repent. They have no desire to avoid the path they are following that will lead them to the Devil.

CHECK THE BOOK

Herod Antipas was the stepfather of the beautiful dancer Salome. Enchanted by her sensuous dancing he offered her half his kingdom, but she asked for the head of John the Baptist on a platter instead. Oscar Wilde's play, *Salome*, was written in 1893. It was first performed in 1896 in Paris, but the English authorities considered it so scandalous that it was not performed on stage in London until 1931.

The Pardoner launches his tirade against drunkenness with a series of references and **allusions** to stories where people have sinned while drunk. He refers to the biblical figure of Lot, who committed the sin of sleeping with his daughter when he was too drunk to realise what he was doing. Also from the Bible, he recounts that Herod only ordered the head of John the Baptist on a platter because he was drunk. The Pardoner's third reference is to the Roman writer Seneca, who wrote that he saw no difference between a madman and drunkard, except that madness tends to last longer than the effects of alcohol.

One can imagine the effect these references would have on a country church congregation of simple, uneducated people. They would assume the Pardoner was a man of great learning who they would do well to listen to (and later give money to). They almost certainly would not know who Seneca was, so the Pardoner returns to the Bible for his fourth reference – Adam. This also signals his progression on to the sin of gluttony as he claims that Adam eating the forbidden apple and causing man's expulsion from the Garden of Eden was a simple example of it. This is not the general view of the meaning of the story. Most clerics of Chaucer's day would have said it showed that Adam was guilty of succumbing to temptation, not gluttony. They would also have said that Adam and Eve's expulsion from the Garden of Eden had more to do with disobeying God's instruction that they should not eat the apple. This suggests that the Pardoner might be happy to distort the meaning of a key story from the Bible to suit his message.

The Pardoner devotes the rest of this section to a vivid and powerful attack on the sin of gluttony. He includes three biblical quotations from St Paul. These provide a contrast to the much more angry, visceral and physical **imagery** expressed in the Pardoner's own words. This reaches maximum **rhetorical** pitch between lines 248–54. The number of exclamation marks suggests he is using heavy emphasis as he delivers his **sermon**. His choice of graphic descriptive words and images convey a powerful sense of disgust and of physical corruption and decay. 'O stinking cod/ Fulfilled of dong and of corrupcioun!' (248–9) is a particularly striking image: the gluttons make their belly a stinking bag of dung and corruption. In the following line he imagines the foul sounds at 'eithere end' of the glutton's body. This is Chaucer at his earthy, bawdy, comic best.

The quotations from St Paul contrast with this tone and underpin it with a more considered criticism of the sin of gluttony. The first (236–7) is from the First Epistle to the Corinthians: 'Meat for the belly, and the belly for the meats: but God shall destroy them both': a reminder that God is greater than anything, including human appetite and sin. The next quote is in line 243, where 'the apostle' is direct reference to St Paul. This time the Pardoner quotes from the Epistle to the Philippians: 'For many walk, of whom I have told you often that they are enemies of the cross of Christ: whose end is destruction: whose God is their belly.' The final quote is (rather loosely) from the First Epistle to Timothy – 'he that haunteth swiche delices/ Is deed, whil that he liveth in tho vices' (261–2): 'For she that liveth in pleasures is dead while she is living'. For the Pardoner's pious listeners, these three quotes provide a solid attack against gluttony from one of the best known figures in the Bible.

CONTEXT

Lucius Annaeus Seneca (died AD 65) was a philosopher and dramatist who wrote in Latin in the first century. He was tutor to the young Roman Emperor Nero, and became one of his chief advisers when Nero came to power. Seneca was accused of participating in a political conspiracy and ordered to take his own life, which he did. He was much admired and studied in the Middle Ages.

CONTEXT

The Pardoner is in fact using a rather obscure version of the symbolism of the forbidden fruit in the Garden of Eden as claimed by St Jerome in his Latin text *Adersus Jovinianum*.

This passage ends with a description of how cooks labour to produce food to satisfy the greedy. But there is no celebration of the arts of good cooking. The Pardoner describes the cooks' work like dirty manual labour: they stamp and strain and grind, as if feeding some gross machine that consumes all they can shovel together for it. Imagine the effect of all this on a simple congregation who probably knew more hungry days than replete ones. It would make them feel blessed that they could not indulge in such excesses and make them hate those who they imagined could do so.

In contrast to the obvious vivid descriptions of over-indulgence that turns the natural and nourishing art of cooking into something physically gross and revolting, line 253 contains a strange image that it is worth looking at in detail. It reveals the depth of meaning and knowledge that Chaucer wrote into many of the Pardoner's utterances.

Having painted a picture of labouring cooks, he says that they 'turnen substaunce into accident' (53). We may read this as a poetic way of saying that, to please the jaded palate of an habitual glutton, cooks make wholesome natural ingredients into 'accidents' of contrived flavour. In fact Chaucer is doing something more complex, which some of his more knowledgeable readers at least would have picked up and enjoyed. This line uses language that was employed in very strict ways by medieval philosophers. They used the term 'accidents' to mean the external appearance of something: its surface colour and texture, for example. 'Substance' for them was the essence of the thing that they supposed underlay what was visible. This idea of the real substance of something being invisible was very important to them. They lived in a world where analysis of physical materials was limited and things existed for them much more on the level of their appearance. The Pardoner suggests that the cooks so completely alter the physical, external qualities of their ingredients that no one can tell what substances are contained in the final dishes – a highly dishonest transformation to attempt.

The theme of corruption – of physical decline and decay not moral or fiscal corruption in the sense of cheating – also pervades this section. Throughout *The Pardoner's Tale* there is constant reference

> **CONTEXT**
> The idea of hell featuring an infernal kitchen where the natural preparation of food becomes distorted into excessive, fiery labour is a common image in literature and painting. Hieronymous Bosch (1450–1516) painted *The Garden of Earthly Delights* which shows the effects of sins including gluttony.

to, or awareness of, the physical decay of both objects and people. Many of the relics the Pardoner mentions are the unpleasant (more so to us than Chaucer's contemporaries, it must be said) residue of physical decay: bones and rags. Chaucer, through the Pardoner, focuses us back to decay, to physical corruption as a theme of the whole text. It matches in physical terms the moral corruption of the Pardoner, and gives the work a dark, **gothic** atmosphere. They remind us that death and decay inevitably follow life.

CHECK THE BOOK

The selling of fake relics also features in the story of Friar Cipollo, contained in the other great medieval collection of tales told by diverse characters, Boccaccio's *Decameron*.

GLOSSARY

200	**doghtres**	daughters
201	**he nyste what he wroghte**	he didn't know what he was doing
204	**yaf his heeste**	gave an order
205	**sleen**	slay
	giltelees	guiltless
209	**dronkelewe**	dead or completely drunk
210	**woodnesse**	madness
	shrewe	a rogue or evil person, not necessarily female, as in later meanings of 'shrew' as a hard-tongued woman
214	**dampnacioun**	damnation
217	**Aboght**	paid for
	thilke	the same
221	**it is no drede**	there is no doubt
224	**deffended**	forbidden
225	**wo and payne**	woe and pain
228	**Folwen**	following from
229	**mesurable**	moderate
231	**shorte throte, the tendre mouth**	a reference to the brief time when food is still in the mouth being tasted, before it descends to the glutton's stomach
233	**men to swinke**	men that labour
234	**deyntee mete**	dainty meat or food.
235	**wel kanstow trete**	as we can know and deal with
241	**privee**	a toilet
242	**Thurgh thilke cursed superfluitee**	through the same cursed excess

continued

CHECK THE POEM

In lines 220–6, the Pardoner identifies the sin of Adam in the Garden of Eden as that of gluttony in taking the apple from Eve. In *Paradise Lost*, Book One (1667), John Milton instead places the blame on the Devil and his sins: 'The infernal Serpent; he it was whose guile / Stirr'd up with envy and revenge deceived / The Mother of mankind' (34–6).

GLOSSARY

245	**vois** voice
248	**cod** bag
254	**likerous talent** greedy desire
256	**mary** (in this case) marrow, as in marrow from a bone
261	**haunteth swiche delices** practices such delights
262	**deed** dead

LINES 263–302

- The Pardoner returns to criticising the sin of drunkenness using the same sort of vivid, earthy images with which he condemned gluttony.

- He employs biblical and **classical allusions** to support his hatred of drinking.

The tone of the writing in this section continues with the pitch and intensity of the previous condemnation of gluttony. The Pardoner demonstrates to the pilgrims his skill as a preacher, his ability to conjure striking images to impress a congregation. This section continues to build the effect of the Pardoner being in 'full cry' in condemning sinfulness. Then, just as a good preacher knows the need for a change in pitch as well as subject matter, he returns to a more measured form of criticism, once again employing biblical and classical allusions.

COMMENTARY

The Pardoner is now in full **rhetorical** mode, showing the pilgrims how he rages in the pulpits of churches to impress on congregations the power of his faith. He pours scorn on drunkenness, and uses strong, crude, physical images (as he did in condemning gluttony) to conjure up the evil physical effects of drinking. Drunkards become disfigured, have foul breath and are horrible to be close to – 'foul artow to embrace' (266). There is a real sense of the Pardoner imagining himself going up close to the face of a glutton or drunk and recoiling from what assails him. The references to Samson, a

CONTEXT

Samson was a wrestler and athlete whose story is told in the Bible in the Book of Judges. He tears down the pillars of a palace where he is asked to perform feats of strength for Philistine princes, destroying them and himself.

biblical figure that most pilgrims and congregations would know
about, turn on the fact that, as a Nazarene, Samson would be
forbidden by his faith to drink, yet his name is used (286) as an
onomatopoeic device to suggest the sibilant breathing of an
unconscious drunk.

The Pardoner employs some brief, vivid images here that both
extend his criticism of drinking and emphasise the way in which he
speaks or preaches. These are focused and conveyed with passion. A
drunk can fall like 'a stiked swyn' (270), a boar run through with a
lance in a hunt. His 'tonge is lost' (271), he cannot speak clearly, and
'He kan no conseil kepe' (275), he cannot keep secrets. The
Pardoner then quietens his fury down a little and goes into what is
really a rather confusing digression (277–85) about wines and where
they come from. Imported Spanish wines are on sale in Fleet Street
or 'Chepe' (Cheapside) (278) – two areas of London – and the
Pardoner claims that when someone has had a glass or two of them
they will believe they are in the country where the wine was made,
not at home in London. Lepe is a wine producing town in Spain; its
wine was of poor quality and was often mixed with better wines and
the blend sold to unsuspecting customers. The Pardoner says the
drunkards will also believe themselves to be in La Rochelle or
Bordeaux, both wine exporting ports. This section seems slightly off
the point and may be inspired by the fact that Chaucer was the son
of a vintner and was himself a customs officer, so he would be well
aware of illegal practices like mixing wines and of how wines were
shipped to London. But it might be fair to say that using this bit of
personal knowledge here rather slows down the otherwise dramatic
drive of the Pardoner's demonstration **sermon**. It does however
provide Chaucer's readers with a little humorous local and current
focus, a break from the lengthy **didactic** sermonising. One or two of
the pilgrims might be wryly recalling that the Pardoner had to have
a drink of '**moiste and corny ale**' (29) before speaking.

However, the Pardoner quickly uses the preacher's rhetorical device
of addressing the pilgrims – and imaginary congregation – directly,
asking them to listen: 'But herkenth, lordyngs, o word I yow preye'
(287). He employs another series of biblical and classical allusions, in
which he claims that all the great victories recorded in the Bible were
won by sober people. Then he reminds the pilgrims that Attila the

**CHECK
THE BOOK**
John Milton's
(1608–74) long
narrative poem
Samson Agonistes
(1671) tells the story
of the last part of
Samson's life.

CONTEXT
The Pardoner's
view of a drinker
being unable to be
discreet can be
contrasted with
the Latin **aphorism**
'*In vino veritas*' –
there is truth in
what is said by one
who is 'in wine'.

CONTEXT

References to Lamuel, also spelt Lemuel in some versions of *The Pardoner's Tale*, can be found in the Bible (Proverbs:31) where the warning is given: 'It is not for kings, O Lemuel, it is not for kings to drink wine; nor for princes strong drink.'

great conqueror expired in a drunken sleep, a shameful way for a hero to die, and Lamuel, also a drunkard, had two wives at the same time, something proscribed by God.

There is a sense that perhaps the Pardoner is losing the momentum of this **sermon**, and recognising this he decides he has said enough about the closely related sins of over-eating and excessive drinking. It is time to move on to another of the sins he imagines the three young men from his story habitually practise: 'hasardrye' (304) or gambling. Chaucer, of course, has total control over the pace and flow of the action, and this is an example of how he skilfully moves readers through the various Tales. He creates a sense of stories being told in an informal social arena, driven by the diverse personalities of their tellers and the expectations, prejudices, tolerance and humour of the listeners.

For further analysis of this section of the Tale, see **Extended commentaries – Text 2**.

GLOSSARY

266	**artow** are you
267	**semeth the soun** the sound seems
268	**seydest** are saying
272	**sepulture** a burial
273	**discrecioun** discretion
281	**swich fumositee** such fumes
283	**weneth** to believe
287	**herkneth** listen
293	**and ther ye may it leere** and there (as in a book) you will learn
294	**Deyde** died
297	**aviseth yow right wel** let you be well advised
301	**wyn-yeving** giving wine

LINES 303–42

- The Pardoner condemns the sin of gambling and the other sins to which it can lead.
- He quotes two examples of the evils of gambling that he ascribes to a book on good governance written by an English cleric.

The Pardoner lists the evils that gambling leads to: double-dealing, lies, manslaughter (when gamblers fall out and fight) and blasphemy. Gambling is a waste of money and destroyer of good reputations. After making these general criticisms, he gives two examples of the evils of gambling taken from (though this reference is not explicitly given by Chaucer) a book on good principles of governance called *The Policratius*.

COMMENTARY

The Pardoner's continues his rhetorical tactic of swapping between angry and quite crude descriptions of the results of sin and more measured use of references to classical and biblical stories to support his themes in this section. The effect is to create a variety of pace and tone, from explicit, furious condemnations to more considered, referenced argument.

The Pardoner makes more rigorous arguments to support his claims through references to other people who have written about the sin of gambling. These references are probably unnecessary for convincing the imagined congregation: perhaps Chaucer allows the Pardoner to do this to expose his vanity. The Pardoner cannot refrain from demonstrating his knowledge of what, even to Chaucer's audience, was a pretty obscure book when, at line 317, he refers to someone called Stilboun, who was an ambassador to Corinth in classical Greece. The Pardoner doesn't mention the text in which he appears, but Chaucer scholars (such as A. C. Spearing in the introduction to the Cambridge edition) have identified it as *The Policratius*. This is a treatise on the principles of good government written (in Latin, a language very few ordinary people could understand) by John of Salisbury, a cleric and scholar, about two hundred years before Chaucer wrote *The Canterbury Tales*.

CONTEXT

John of Salisbury (died 1180) was present in Canterbury Cathedral when Thomas à Becket was murdered. He later wrote 'Entheticus', an **elegiac** poem in praise of the martyr.

CONTEXT
Parthia was a country located in the north of present day Iraq, which appears to have been at its height from approximately 248 BC to AD 10, when the traditionally nomadic Parthians settled lands between the Indus and Euphrates rivers.

In his book, John tells the story of how Stilboun was sent by his country, the austere and warlike Sparta, to Corinth, a neighbouring state in what is now modern Greece. He was to negotiate a treaty of alliance. Stilboun found the Corinthians busy playing dice. This so enraged his sense of honour that he left Corinth saying he would not stain the honour of his country by making a treaty with gamblers. The Pardoner thinks this was the right thing to do, and stays with *The Policratius* to quote another example from antiquity about gambling being something that destroys personal honour. The King of Parthia wanted to insult King Demetrius and the most effective way he could devise of doing this was to send him a pair of golden dice, suggesting that he was an inveterate gambler.

Throughout the Prologue and Tale, Chaucer, through the Pardoner, makes many **allusions** to classical stories and the Bible. Sometimes we can grasp the general sense of a passage even if we don't understand the references. At other times we need to understand them to see what Chaucer/the Pardoner is saying. Sometimes, as befits a man who was regarded as one of the most widely read and knowledgeable of his time, Chaucer's references can be very obscure, both to us and probably to many of his less well-educated contemporaries. However, not knowing his sources does not detract from the flow, impact and meaning of his writing.

CONTEXT
The universities of Oxford and Cambridge were both in existence by Chaucer's time, and though men studied a range of subjects there, all students were required also to train to be priests. Women were not admitted.

The sum of human knowledge that could be learned from books in medieval England was much smaller than today. There were far fewer books in existence, and it was possible for one person to have a general understanding of all the major areas of human enquiry and creativity. Crucially, overarching all the knowledge that was available to a scholar or reader – in Europe at least – in the Middle Ages, was the intellectual and spiritual primacy of Christian thought, stories, church dogma and history. The fact that almost every person in England was to some extent a practising Christian meant that faith-based stories and references were a common intellectual source of shared knowledge; the Church at that time incorporated many stories from the Old Testament of the Bible into much of its theology and preaching so most people were to some extent conversant in the stories and rules of the Christian faith (for more on this subject see **Language and style: Allusion**).

GLOSSARY

304	**now wol I yow deffenden hasardrye** now I will forbid you to gamble
305	**mooder of lesinges** mother of lies
306	**forsweringes** perjuries (false claims)
307	**wast** waste
308	**catel** goods or riches
309	**repreeve** shame
310	**a commune hasardour** a common and notorious gambler
316	**Yholde the lasse in reputacioun** you will have less reputation
324	**He stal him hoom** he stole away secretly home
329	**me were levere die** I would more willingly die
330	**allye** make alliance with
333	**tretee** diplomacy
337	**dees of gold** gold dice
338	**For he hadde used hasard ther-biforn** because he had previously indulged in gambling
341	**maner play** other ways to play or pass the time
342	**to drive the day awey** to make the day pass (in activity)

LINES 343–73

- The Pardoner attacks another of the vices indulged in by the 'compaignye of yonge folke': swearing and its related sin, perjury.

- He claims swearing is a terrible sin and quotes several blasphemies as if spoken by people playing a game of chance.

This final section of the Pardoner's lengthy demonstration **sermon** follows the pattern he has established throughout, of simple and direct condemnation contrasting with 'learned' **allusions** and references. Perhaps anticipating the conclusion of his tirade against the sins that the young men in the long-delayed story exhibit, most

 CHECK THE BOOK

The Medieval Craft of Memory: An Anthology of Texts and Pictures, Mary Carruthers and Jan Ziolkowski, (Editors), (University of Pennsylvania Press, 2002) will give you an insight into both the text of sermons and the theology that underpinned them.

of this section is closely tied to biblical and Christian references. He closes this section by vividly creating the anger and oaths of someone he imagines engaged in a furious game of dice.

COMMENTARY

We might think that the pilgrims would be wondering what has happened to the story the Pardoner began and then abandoned. However, the idea behind telling the Tales was to while away the journey, so Chaucer is balancing the need to drive the narrative of each Tale forward, in order to keep his readers' attention, while retaining the idea that the Tales were being spun to pass long hours on the road. We can accept that the pilgrims, with no other distractions all day, and being used to hearing lengthy sermons in church, would indulge the Pardoner during his extensive attack on various sins. Others might applaud the apparent piety of his words while some might see the whole hypocritical tirade as satire, and be laughing at his deliberate excesses. To us, the Pardoner's lengthy sermonising might seem an overlong delay before the Tale itself, but this sermon would have far more entertainment value to Chaucer's pilgrims than we might expect.

The Pardoner says that 'grete' swearing and cursing, the use of foul language when annoyed or excited is bad (345), but 'fals swering' – the telling of lies under oath – is worse, 'yet moore reprevable' or shameful (346). This is a different use of the term 'swearing' to that which we would usually understand today, more akin to perjury. Perjury is swearing under oath to tell the truth (as in a court of law) but then failing to do so.

The references the Pardoner now employs are all to biblical and Christian stories that he could safely assume would be familiar to almost all the pilgrims. He refers to Jeremiah's warning against swearing as recorded by St Matthew in his gospel. The 'firste table' the Pardoner mentions (35) is the first of the two tablets of stone which Moses brought down from the mountain with five of the Ten Commandments written on each of them.

The Pardoner makes the somewhat convoluted claim that swearing is worse than murder because it is prohibited by 'seconde heeste'

(355) or the second of the Ten Commandments – 'Thou shalt not take the name of the Lord your God in vain' – while 'Thou shalt not commit murder' is only ranked sixth. In fact, scholars and believers do not regard the Ten Commandments as having any ranking order. It might be thought that the Pardoner is rather twisting things here. He is making a case for a sin he needs to criticise being worse than one – murder – that most people would argue is obviously far more reprehensible than swearing.

The final section of the Pardoner's tirade against swearing is a lively, imagined game of dice where a player commits four rapid blasphemies, including a rather obscure one invoking 'the blood of Crist that is in Hayles' (366). This, appropriately given the Pardoner's profession, refers to a once greatly-venerated holy relic: a phial or small capsule supposedly containing some of Christ's blood, which was kept at Hailes Abbey in Gloucestershire. This relic made the Abbey a famous site of pilgrimage in Chaucer's time. The relic was publicly destroyed by Henry VIII when he dissolved the monasteries in the sixteenth century.

In the popular dice game of Hazard, a 'chaunce' (367) is a throw which neither loses or wins, but gives the player another turn. The references to 'cynk' and 'treye' are to the numbers two and three on the dice (367). *The Canterbury Tales* tries to present all of life, and here Chaucer goes from biblical references to the rules of gambling in one short passage. This shows the wide range of Chaucer's knowledge and skill as a writer. The passage also exemplifies a key element of the Pardoner's skill as a preacher: to present to congregations vivid images and scenes that they can imagine. He provides a graphic commentary to the sinful scene: the violent threat of a dagger through the heart from one player is quoted (369) and the dice are described as 'bicched bones two' (370), or cursed bones, as they would most probably have been made of bone. This powerfully expressive passage, with its final list of the evils that attend gambling (371), is the last **rhetorical** 'peak' of the Pardoner's demonstration **sermon**. We can imagine him pausing for effect before at last telling the pilgrims that he will now return to his story.

CONTEXT
The Ten Commandments are arranged in a different order by the Catholic and Protestant churches. 'Thou shalt not take the name of the Lord your God in vain' is the second commandment in the Catholic order, but third in the Protestant.

CONTEXT
Henry VIII, King of England (1509–47), fell out with the Catholic Church in Rome over his wish to divorce his first wife, Catherine of Aragon. He rejected Papal supremacy and suppressed the Catholic faith in England. He closed or dissolved all the Catholic monasteries and other religious orders.

GLOSSARY

346	**reprevable** shameful
350	**swere sooth thine othes** swear only true oaths
351	**eek in rightwisnesse** also in righteousness
354	**heestes honurable** honourable commandments
356	**in idel or amis** in vain or wrongly
359	**stondeth** stands
362	**I wol thee telle al plat** I will tell you plainly
368	**Goddes armes** by God's arms, a curse
370	**This fruit cometh of the bicched bones two** this outcome results from two cursed bones (dice)

LINES 374–424

- The Pardoner begins his Tale, describing how three sinful young men were sitting in a tavern when they saw a funeral go by.

- When they learn that the deceased has been killed while drunk, by a thief called Death, they decide to find Death and murder him.

- The publican warns them that Death has already killed many people.

- The three drunks swear an oath together and set off to find Death.

The Pardoner tells how in Flanders at the height of the Black Death three sinners, probably from the same 'compaignye of yonge folk' (177) he spoke of at the start of his Tale, are in a tavern, drunk as usual. They see a funeral go past and learn from a boy who works in the tavern that the dead man was someone they knew who was killed the night before by a thief called Death. The publican says that Death has killed many people in a nearby village. The three men vow like brothers to one another that together they will go off and kill this terrible thief called Death.

CONTEXT

The **personification** of Death as a grim figure stalking the land claiming souls was a key aspect of art and of popular belief through the Middle Ages. Now mostly a caricature figure in a black cloak carrying a scythe, he was a real fear for most people in Chaucer's time.

COMMENTARY

Now that the Pardoner has started on his actual Tale, it is quickly and vividly told. He does not spend time adding any details that aren't strictly necessary to the unfolding events. For example, we get no picture of the physical appearance of the three men, nor of the tavern in which they are located. Chaucer is a master of controlling the pace and flow of the stories and here, within one relatively short Tale, we move from a lengthy **sermon**, where the chief pleasure for his readers was in seeing how the Pardoner preached so extensively on well-known themes, to a rapid unfolding of a plot-driven story.

It is early morning in the Flanders countryside and already the three young men are drinking in the village tavern. The Pardoner says it is 'Longe erst er prime rong of any belle' (376), long before any bell has been rung for the church service of Prime, one of the times appointed by the Church for prayer. Usually only attended by monks and nuns in religious communities, Prime is celebrated at about six o'clock in the morning. We might assume therefore that the three men have been in the tavern all night.

Plague is devastating the countryside. A funeral passes by, and here the Pardoner does sketch in sufficient detail to give the scene an air of melancholy. They men hear a bell 'clinke' (378) and the funeral itself is described coldly as a corpse being carried to the grave. They tell the tavern serving boy to go and find out who has died.

Free from the need to digress into quotations, the language of the Tale is now more focused on to plain description, **dialogue** and storytelling. The use of direct speech between the young men, the serving 'knave', (young boy) (381) and the 'taverner' (399) gives the telling of the story an immediacy that contrasts with the style of the sermon we have just heard. We can imagine the innkeeper coming over to join in the conversation when he says 'By seinte Marie/ … The child seith sooth' (399–400), before describing how death has ravaged a nearby 'greet village' (401). Then one of the drunken young men jumps into the conversation with another blasphemous curse: 'Ye, Goddes armes! / … Is it swich peril with him for to meete?' (406–7).

> **CONTEXT**
>
> Although the Tale is set in some unspecified 'long ago', the Plague Chaucer is imagining is the Black Death, which had appeared in England in 1349 and again in 1361. A variant of typhus, it turned the body black in a process of rapid putrefaction and killed twenty-five million people across Europe.

The boy says he has no need to go and ask, because he has in the last two hours been told that the deceased was a friend of the three men. He was killed last night while he lay drunk on his bench by 'a privee theef men cleped Deeth' (389). The pestilence that the boy refers to is the Black Death, a plague raging across Flanders killing many people. To modern ears the logic of this doesn't work. Why don't the three men know that their friend has been killed by the plague? Why don't they see that the boy is, to use modern terms, speaking **metaphorically** and is, note the upper case 'D' in the first mention of 'Deeth' (389), **personifying** Death, calling him a thief of people's lives? The answer is that this is not supposed to be a Tale that could realistically be imagined to happen in real life: it is more like a fable. It is designed purely to illustrate the Pardoner's theme in a graphic and engaging way.

The boy says that Death is everywhere; he has killed a thousand people already. He is a terrible adversary. The taverner, or publican, joins in, saying that in a nearby village Death killed everyone who lived there: men, women and children. He believes that Death has made that village his home , his 'habitacioun' (403). It is not clear whether the boy and the taverner think of death as a person as the young men do, but the idea of Death personified and nearby is a very gothic notion. Dramatically, the purpose of the taverner's words is to cast a supernatural shadow over the debauched but otherwise everyday scene.

CHECK THE BOOK

The story *The Werewolf* in Angela Carter's collection of darkly **gothic** tales *The Bloody Chamber* (Vintage, 1979) uses the idea of the devil abroad in the land to create a haunting sense of terror. For the woodsmen in the story 'the devil is as real as you or I' and they glimpse him often in graveyards.

One of the young men, a 'riotour' (rioter) utters a blasphemy, 'Ye, Goddes armes' (406) and, far from being frightened by what he has heard, vows to search the streets to find Death. He utters another curse that abuses the name of God – 'I make avow to Goddes digne bones' (409), before getting his two friends to swear an oath together 'like brothers'. Before nightfall they will find and slay this 'false traitor' who has killed so many of their friends. This passage is full of energy and vigour. The men's oaths may be drink-fuelled, but they are full of passion. As ever, the use of direct speech adds energy to the poetry.

This section concludes with the claim that when they have finished 'deeth shall be deed' (424). It is a nonsensical statement, perhaps reflecting the fact that they are too drunk to think straight. It is however interesting to note that this plan is apparently selfless. They are not going to kill Death for personal gain, but to save their world from a terrible scourge, and possibly to avenge their deceased friend. It may be fair to say that the three drunken men at least set off from the tavern with good, almost charitable, intentions.

The oaths that the men swear throughout this section, the blasphemous oaths the Pardoner quotes and the oath with which the Host starts the Introduction, all refer to Christ's body: his blood from his wounds at the crucifixion and bones, for example. This degree of reference to the body of Christ may strike us as obsessive but the physicality of Christ was a key part of the Catholic way of thinking in Chaucer's time. Religion, as has been noted elsewhere, was much more focused on material things than on to ideas and Chaucer's choice of blasphemous oaths reflects this.

CONTEXT

The idea of the bodily nature of God, the physical presence of religious power, has at its core the Catholic notion of transubstantiation, whereby at every Mass the bread and wine, according to the believer, *become* the blood and body of Christ. In the Protestant Church of England, the bread and wine of Communion *symbolise* the body and blood of Christ.

GLOSSARY

379   **Biforn a cors** before a corpse
380   **oon of hem** one of them
      knave here this means a serving boy in the tavern
381   **axe** ask
382   **forby** past, as in going past
384   **never-a-deel** not at all
385   **It was me toold er ye cam** I was told before you came
386   **pardee** indeed
      old felawe companion
387   **sodeynly** suddenly
388   **Fordronke** absolutely drunk
389   **privee** (as used here) secret
      clepeth call
390   **contree** country
      sleeth kills
391   **spere** spear

continued

GLOSSARY

396	**For to be war** to beware
398	**my dame** my mother
400	**seith sooth** tell the truth
402	**Henne** a labourer
408	**by wey and eek by strete** by way and by street
409	**Goddes digne bones** God's noble bones, a curse
414	**he that so manye sleeth** he that has killed so many
416	**Togidres han thise thre hir trouthe plight** together these three pledged together
418	**owene ybore brother** own born brother
419	**stirte** stirred, jumped up
423	**Cristes blessed body al torente** Christ's blessed body all torn to pieces
424	**if that they may him hente** if they can catch or seize him

LINES 425–519

- The three men set off and meet a mysterious old man whom they treat contemptuously.
- He tells them he wants to die but is unable to.
- One of the young men accuses the old man of being Death's spy.
- The old man says he saw Death under a tree just along the way.
- The three men go there and find a great pile of gold florins.
- They draw lots to choose one of them to go into town and bring back food and drink.

The three drunken young men meet an old man who says he has wandered far and wide looking for someone to swap their youth for his old age. No one will and now he is so old he longs for Death. He says that he has met Death and even he refused to take him. The young men treat the old man rudely and threaten him. They demand to know where Death is. He tells them he is nearby under a tree. When the young men get to the tree they find a pile of gold

CONTEXT

Medieval artists often painted pictures that showed vivid aspects of the battle between God and the Devil. Often these were based on **allegorical** themes and are alive with devils and angels in vicious combat. Hans Holbein the Younger (1497–1543), an artist who worked just after the medieval period, developed this style of painting. His *Dance of Death* series features many grim, allegorical images. One of the most striking is *The Gambler*, showing a man dragged from the gaming table by Death (a skeleton) and a demon.

coins. The plan to kill Death is forgotten in an instant. They decide to wait and move the treasure at night. They draw lots to choose one of them to go and get food and drink to help them wait for nightfall. The youngest of the three draws the short straw and heads into town.

COMMENTARY

Now the Pardoner pushes events forward at a great pace. The three men leave the tavern and within half a mile come across an old man. Again, he is a type rather than a character in the sense that we would expect to find in modern literature. He is mysterious, nameless and his sole purpose in the Tale is to convey a crucial message and move the plot forward. Many critics see him as the **personification** of death. Or perhaps he is a supernatural agent of death, just as the Devil was imagined in the Middle Ages to be attended by countless demons and other evil creatures.

If he is Death himself, then of course the old man is lying to the three men throughout, and is setting them a trap when he tells them where they can find Death. Chaucer says that the young men meet the old man at a stile (426), a nice detail that emphasises the rural setting of the encounter.

Extensive use of direct speech creates a sense of dramatic dialogue, and even though each speaker delivers quite long speeches, we hear the difference between the rude, threatening young men and the polite and humble old man. Reading more carefully, however, we see how he becomes more mysterious in what he says. He expresses a pitiful though unusual human condition, his apparent unwished-for immortality which is especially surprising in this time of rampant plague. Of course there is something more behind his words, something that the drunken young men miss or ignore. Again a sense of gothic darkness is cast across the Tale: why would the old man expect anyone to swap their youth for his age, and, more mysteriously, why has death refused to take this ancient man? Discounting the notion that he is Death himself, is he the victim of some curse that forces eternal old age upon him?

From the very start of their meeting, the young men are rude to the old man. They wonder why he is so wrapped up that nothing but

CHECK THE BOOK

Bram Stoker's **gothic** masterpiece *Dracula* (1897) established the myth that vampires cannot die unless killed in very specific ways. Later variants of the basic Dracula story have focused on the undead Count wishing for death but being unable to leave his shadowy vampire existence.

his face is visible. They never stop to think that this may be to hide his true identity – for if he were Death, then his body, as many medieval artists imagined it, would be a mere skeleton. Casting a gothic mood over this meeting, we might imagine that Death has to cover the fact that he is not human. The mention of 'Inde' (436) may sound odd to us, but in medieval poetry this was a common phrase meaning something like 'the ends of the earth'.

The old man longs to die but even Death will not take him. The Pardoner presents us with the pitiful image of the old man knocking with his stick on the earth asking to be taken in (to die and be buried). He calls upon the earth as his mother, a clear example of **personification**, though one which, with its overtones of 'earth mother' or 'mother nature' sounds more pagan than Christian. If the young men were not so drunk perhaps they would stop and consider why in a time of plague, the old man is apparently immune to infection. He wanders everywhere but is unable to die. At lines 448–50 he wishes he could exchange the chest that has for so long been in his chamber for a 'clowte', a shroud, to wrap himself in.

He is possessed by his own misery but not so much that he is unaware of the attitude of the three young men. He tells them that in the presence of an old, white-haired man, they should, as 'Hooly Writ' demands, 'arise' (468–9). He means they should do this **metaphorically**, for they are already on their feet, as a mark of respect before an old man like him. He quotes from the Bible to the young men, Leviticus 19:32, 'Rise up before the hoary head, and honour the person of the aged man'. He is not afraid to make this point to them.

The old man concludes his speech by again invoking the name of God in a positive and to Chaucer's audience acceptable (non-blaspheming) way – 'God be with yow' (462). The contrast between how he and the young men use the name of God could not be stronger, and this sets up a tension that gives this passage more drama. Furthermore, having provided very specific instructions as to where to find death, the old man's departure leaves a further mystery that the three young men fail to notice: he says has a destination to travel to, but he does not say what or where this is.

CHECK THE BOOK
The stories of Edgar Allan Poe (1811–49) are driven by strong **gothic** elements. *The Masque of the Red Death* (1842) has parallels with the meeting between the young men and the old man. In Poe's story people try to hide from Death; like the young men they engage in debauched behaviour, and in the end Death comes for them.

Critics have spent a long time puzzling over the identity of the old man and exactly what he is supposed to be or represent in the Tale. What is his intention: to warn the young men that their lives are in danger? If so, he doesn't, as we might expect, suggest that their sinful ways might lead them to destruction. What if he is Death personified? If he is, why does he voice such a long and very human complaint about his inability to die? In similar stories derived from folk legends, mysterious characters, like the old man, often act as providers of direful warnings to protagonists, or as guardians to frontiers that travellers are cautioned not to cross. Perhaps the old man could be an example of another standard type of folkloric or mythic character: the figure cursed for eternity as a result of misdeeds. Is the old man cursed with endless old age because of a misspent youth, because of sins he has committed?

There is no indication that this old man is empowered to utter special warnings, nor that he is cursed to endure endless old age because of misdeeds, nor is there any explanation for his piteous condition. Apart from the three young men, he is the only other significant character in the story, yet he is a great enigma. While his identity is unclear, the important thing is the contrast between him and the young men. He is humble, they are arrogant. He invokes the name of God as a source of comfort and strength, they blaspheme. He searches for death/Death but (we assume) doesn't find it/him. These lead to the final contrast of the story: the young men search for Death personified to kill him, but bring about their own deaths instead.

The three young men run off to the tree in the grove where the old man said he saw Death, where they find a pile of gold coins. All thoughts of committing an act of revenge for their dead friend by murdering Death immediately vanish. Instead, the youngest of them says that this pile of 'well nigh' eight bushels (a unit of cubic measurement) of newly minted gold florins must have been left there for them by Fortune. (Note the capital 'F'; like Death, Fortune is personified.) They never consider that it might be a trap or that it could be someone else's property. Here again they swear by using God's name – 'Goddes precious dignitee' (496). Not strictly a blasphemy perhaps, and not said in anger, but not particularly reverential nonetheless.

> **CONTEXT**
>
> Many fairy tales begin with warnings from some figure of authority to people not to go into the woods. In medieval England, woods covered much of the country and were generally regarded as places of potential lawlessness and danger. For many of Chaucer's audience, such warnings given in a fiction would echo their own experiences.

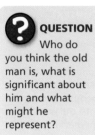

QUESTION

Who do you think the old man is, what is significant about him and what might he represent?

The habitual blaspheming of the three young men throughout this passage reminds the Pardoner's listeners that, as well as their main sin of avarice, they are constantly committing the sin of 'taking the Lord God's name in vain' (Exodus 20:1). The Pardoner needs to create a sense that they are building an ever-increasing catalogue of sins that sooner or later will be paid back by some kind of downfall. It was an absolute belief for Chaucer's audience that sin never went unpunished. When sinners did apparently live their entire lives without suffering for their actions – or even appeared to prosper by them – theologians and churchmen made it clear that these sinners would get their punishment in the next life, possibly for all eternity in hell.

This section of the story has been full of dramatic action accompanied by rapid changes of tone in its direct speech: the angry words of the young men to the old man, his bitter complaints about his inability to find Death and his humble replies to the young men; and finally the happy conversation between the three men who are delighted to have discovered treasure.

GLOSSARY

427	**povre**	poor
428	**grette**	greet
431	**carl**	fellow
432	**artow**	art thou, are you
433	**livestow**	do you live
435	**I ne kan net finde**	I cannot find
439	**moot**	may or must
442	**kaitif**	captive, a prisoner
443	**moodres gate**	my mother's gate
450	**heyre clowt**	a haircloth rag
454	**vileynye**	villainy, as in harm or wrong
456	**ye may yourself wel rede**	you may well read there
458	**I yeve yow reed**	I give you advice
464	**cherl**	villain
469	**espye**	a spy
470	**or thou shalt it abye**	or you will pay for
474	**if yow be so leef**	if you wish

GLOSSARY

476	**by my fey**	by my faith
478	**Noght for youre boost**	nothing for your boasting
482	**everich**	each one, each of them
491	**taak kep what that I seye**	take notice of what I say
492	**bourde**	joke
496	**who wende**	who travels or journeys
501	**in heigh felicitee**	in high or great happiness
504	**honge**	hang, as in be hanged
507	**rede**	a reed or straw
510	**renne**	run
516	**That oon of hem the cut broghte in his fest** the one who had cut (the straws) brought up his fist (with them in it)

LINES 520–608

- The two young men guarding the gold agree a plan to kill the third when he returns.

- The third young man buys poison and puts it into the wine he brings back for the other two, in order to kill them and keep all the treasure for himself.

- The two men who guarded the treasure kill their friend, and then drink the poisoned wine, leading to their death.

The 'friends' show just how deeply sunk into sin they are by their readiness to murder one another to gain a bigger share of the treasure. The two left guarding it agree to kill the third in a 'playful' wrestle when he returns from town with the food and drink, while he plans to poison the wine he brings back for them. He buys poison and three bottles, two of which he fills with poisoned wine. When he returns the others leap on him and kill him, then drink the poisoned wine and die. The **moral tale** has reached its satisfying conclusion: all three sinners have found Death, but not in the way they intended when they set out from the tavern.

CONTEXT
The method of making a choice as to who will undertake a task by the drawing of straws, one of which is shorter than the others and signifies that its drawer is the chosen one, is the one used by the Host in *The General Prologue* to decide who tells the first story.

CHECK THE FILM

The Pardoner's Tale (2007, directed by Dan Olson) resets the Tale to modern day Montana in America. It is a low budget 'art house' film that is available on DVD. It deviates from the pure form of Chaucer's Tale and suffers from the problem that many modern re-workings encounter: how to create an effective equivalent character for the Pardoner in modern secular society.

COMMENTARY

The overall purpose of this section is to move the plot swiftly on and to show how little the 'friends' value one another. 'No honour amongst thieves' might very well sum up the theme of this section of the story. The Pardoner himself acknowledges (593) that the unfolding actions need no further explanation: they speak for themselves. The theme of deception which runs through the whole of *The Pardoner's Tale* at several different levels is the cause of the three men's deaths (see **Themes: Deception**).

Many critics regard the Tale of these three men as one of the best short stories ever written. It is not long, it is atmospheric, focused on developing a big theme, and has a satisfying twist in its conclusion. It is a story that existed in diverse forms in the canon of folk stories and legends long before Chaucer created this version. The core idea of it has been used as the basis for many more modern versions.

The Pardoner as storyteller skilfully balances the need for sufficient detail to create a convincing story with the need for a rapid pace moving towards a conclusion. He gives enough of the speech between the two men left guarding the treasure to show not just the mechanics of the unfolding plot, but also how the one who suggests the murder hypocritically uses the same terms of friendship to justify the plan as they all used together when vowing to kill Death.

One of the two men left to guard the treasure sets about convincing the other, from line 521, that a good plan would be to kill the third when he comes back. Then they only have to divide the coins two ways. The manner in which he sets about suggesting his plan is interesting. He starts by saying that his friend knows that he his 'sworn brother' (521), and that if he could suggest a way of increasing their shares of the treasure, wouldn't that be the act of a good friend? The speaker is claiming exactly the sort of loyalty he is abusing by suggesting they kill the third member of their gang. It is a great display of hypocrisy, designed to increase our contempt for these two men.

The Pardoner introduces the idea of the 'feend' (558), the Devil, entering the man's head and suggesting the idea of poisoning the wine. To us, this might seem as if he is offering a glimpse of an excuse for the young man's treachery: that it was the devil who corrupted his otherwise possibly honest intentions. For people of Chaucer's time, however, their view of evil and temptation was different. We focus much more on personal moral commitment and self-control, whereas for them the Devil was real. You would suffer damnation for the evil acts he encouraged you to commit. He would literally make you sin then take your soul to hell. Thus evil acts would have two levels of effect: the practical misery they caused on earth and the eternal damnation of the soul of those who caused them. Here, the assumption is that the fiend may be ready to tempt the young man to commit murder, but a less sinful person would have the strength to resist his advances.

Whether it is his own evil cunning or the Devil entering his thoughts, when the young man gets to the town he goes straight to an apothecary. He says he has rats and a polecat in his yard that are killing his 'capouns' (570), chickens, and needs to poison them. The apothecary sells him a poison that he says will kill any living creature who eats even just a grain of food poisoned with it. Before they have had the time to walk a mile – 'goon a paas not but a mile' (580) – they will be dead. Chaucer gives us an intriguing insight into the reality of medieval life (if indeed he is reflecting real situations in the Tale) when he assumes his audience would understand the ready availability of lethal poison from the local town apothecary.

The young man then finds someone to sell him three bottles. He puts poisoned wine in two, pure wine for himself into the third. (He knows that without the help of his friends he will be working all night moving the heap of coins.) He then heads back to his waiting friends. The Pardoner has provided all the practical details of the plot neatly and quickly, keeping the narrative drive of the unfolding plot moving forward while leaving no loose threads in the plan.

The Pardoner uses a **rhetorical** question addressed to the pilgrims to introduce the quick final **denouement** of the story. 'What nedeth it to sermone of it moore?' (593) suggests that the final act of the

 CHECK THE BOOK
At the end of Shakespeare's great tragedy *Hamlet*, Laertes, Hamlet's sworn enemy, suggests a sporting duel before the court, but he ensures that the tip of his sword is sharpened (not blunted as it should be for such contests) and dipped in poison. Like the three men in *The Pardoner's Tale*, the plan misfires and both Hamlet and Laertes are fatally wounded by the lethal sword.

CHECK THE BOOK

An apothecary has an important role to play in Shakespeare's *Romeo and Juliet* – he supplies Romeo with poison, which the young hero uses to kill himself.

story needs no additional **sermon** on the theme of love of money causing evil. Events speak for themselves.

We might ask 'But what happened to the treasure, and to the old man?' but as far as the Pardoner is concerned the story is over. Its whole purpose was to illustrate the text 'Love of money is the root of all evil', and that has been achieved in a satisfying and entertaining way.

Even at this dramatically climatic point in his Tale, the Pardoner cannot forebear from using references to embellish his meaning. 'Avycen' (603) is a reference to Avicenna, the Latinised spelling of the name of Ibn Sina, a great Arabic philosopher and scientist. He was well-known in the West for his writings on medicine. The reference to 'fen' (604) is to Sina's best-known work, *The Book of the Canon in Medicine*, which was divided into sections called (in translation) 'fens'. The point the Pardoner is making is that this case of poisoning is so perfect that Sina never wrote of a better example: 'Wroot nevere in no canon, ne in no fen, /Mo wonder signes of empoisoning' (604–5).

For further analysis of this section of the Tale, see **Extended commentaries – Text 3**.

GLOSSARY	
524	**felawe** our fellow, our friend
529	**a freendes torn** a friend's (good) turn
533	**Shal it be conseil** shall it be a secret
542	**rive him thurgh the sides tweye** stab him twice in the side
543	**strongelest** struggle
545	**departed be** be divided between
550	**thriddle** third
561	**For-why** because
	swich livinge living such a life
563	**outrely** truly
566	**pothecarie** an apothecary, forerunner of a pharmacist
570	**capouns** capons or chickens

GLOSSARY

576	**confiture** a preparation
577	**montance of a corn of whete** an amount no bigger than a grain of wheat
588	**he shoop him for to swinke** he planned to labour or work
594	**hadde cast his deeth bifoore** had planned his death already
599	**par cas** by chance
601	**yaf** gave

LINES 609–82

- The Pardoner lists again the sins of the three men and tries to sell his pardons to the pilgrims.

- He suggests they buy pardons to ensure they are in a State of Grace in case they have a fatal accident on the road.

- When he calls the Host to be the first to pay for a pardon, the Host becomes angry and insults the Pardoner in a vulgar and furious manner.

- The Knight intervenes to restore calm.

The Pardoner reviews the sins of the three men and wonders how mortal man can have become so removed from God's grace. He then begins an attempt to offer relics and pardons to his fellow pilgrims, specifically pardons for the sin of avarice. By stressing the need for them to pay for each pardon, he is demonstrating, without apparent irony or self-awareness, how he is guilty of that very sin. He moves on to offering pardons generally, especially to ensure the pilgrims will be in a State of Grace if a fatal accident should befall them on the road. He stresses even more strongly the need for the pilgrims to pay for them. He suggests they could even buy a new pardon for every mile they travel. When he encourages the Host to be the first to open his purse, the Host replies with vulgarity and aggression, threatening to cut off the Pardoner's testicles. The Knight steps in and restores calm between the two men, and the company of pilgrims continue on their way.

CONTEXT

For Catholics it is important to die in a 'State of Grace', that is with all your past sins absolved or pardoned. Usually this is achieved by confessing sins to a priest. Catholics believe that if you die without being in a State of Grace, your journey to heaven is impeded.

CONTEXT

The seven deadly sins are the seven 'cardinal' or 'mortal sins', as identified by the Catholic Church. The Church specifies two types of sins: venial or minor ones, and cardinal ones, the practice of which leads to damnation. The seven cardinal sins are lust, gluttony, greed, sloth, wrath, envy and pride.

COMMENTARY

The Pardoner quickly reviews all the sins the three men committed (609–11) and wonders how man, for whom Christ died, can become so false and unkind. The number of exclamation marks in these few lines suggests a very forceful and energetic final denouncement of sin. The pilgrims might see this as being a fitting way further to draw the moral purpose out of the story. In fact, this is the Pardoner's first 'introduction' to his plan to offer pardons and relics to his fellow-pilgrims. Remember, the whole of *The Pardoner's Tale* (the confession, **sermon** and the Tale itself) is being presented by him to the pilgrims as an example of how good he is as a preacher and seller of pardons. We can imagine the pilgrims, still thinking about his entertaining story, gradually realising that the Pardoner is aiming his 'pitch' at them and becoming more and more frustrated with him – and with the implicit criticism of them in what he is saying (that they too are sinners in need of pardon).

At first the Pardoner continues to quote what he says to congregations when he is preaching (608–29). After telling such a Tale as the pilgrims have just heard, his trick is then to exhort people to come forward to purchase holy pardons. His 'sales pitch' is relentless and far removed from any moral quality he might have exhibited in telling the story. His absolute personal commitment to the sin of avarice shines through his appeal. If people haven't got money, 'nobles', gold coins, or 'sterlinges', silver pennies (621) they can give brooches, spoons, rings; wives can give wool (that presumably they spin to make money). There is a desperate greed in his words. He brings this harangue to a sudden halt by saying 'And lo, sires, thus I preche' (629). The show is over.

Then, as so often happens throughout *The Pardoner's Tale*, there is a sudden change of direction and focus. There is a surprising moment of apparent honesty and clarity at lines 629–32. Here the Pardoner seems to be saying in a heartfelt way that though he has given what he thinks is a powerful demonstration of his ability to preach against sin, in the end only 'Jhesu Crist' (630) can grant anyone a genuine pardon. The Pardoner says that he cannot really grant pardons, and he does not wish to deceive the pilgrims. If so much in his Prologue and Tale is about deception and appearance disguising true nature and intent, here, just for a moment, there appears to be total honesty.

This clarity doesn't last long. It is as if the Pardoner cannot help himself from continuing in the way he habitually operates, for he now tries to sell the pilgrims the very pardons he has previously delighted in showing to be fake. He begins by assuming that the pilgrims must be guilty of the sin of avarice and he offers pardons specifically for this. Of course by selling these, he is ready to commit exactly the sin he is offering to pardon. He then moves on to the various relics he has in his 'male' (bag) (634), and tries to get the pilgrims to buy these. His claims become excessive: he says he has pardons and relics given to him by the Pope's hand (636). It is highly unlikely that the highest spiritual authority in the Christian world would have personally given him relics to sell. He is offering to wipe away all sins – for a price.

The Pardoner picks the wrong person to ask to be the first to open their purse when he invites the lusty and blunt Host to pay to kiss his holy relics. It doesn't help that the Pardoner says he has chosen the Host to be first because he is the most 'envoluped' in 'sinne' (656): presumably he assumes this because of the Host's profession as a landlord. The Host doesn't mention the notion of buying pardons. His response is much more earthy, imaginatively vulgar and perfectly in character. He suggests that instead of paying for the privilege of kissing 'thyn old breech' (662), some rag the Pardoner claims is a saint's relic which is in fact stained by the Pardoner's own backside, he would rather have the Pardoner's testicles, 'coillons' (666) in his hands. He would cut them off and enshrine them in a hog's turd! The Host's use of the verb 'shrined' (669) plays on the idea that valued relics were often enshrined in costly and ornate cases to be displayed in churches: here he creates a vulgar, **scatological** parallel.

The Pardoner is struck dumb by the Host's crude assault. The Knight, seeing everyone laughing – a small detail that suggests the Pardoner is not well liked, as well as showing the pilgrims' easy ability to switch from contemplating a **moral tale** to laughing at extreme vulgarity – intervenes and makes the Host and Pardoner 'kisse' (679). Before he can intervene, however, the Host says rather

> **CONTEXT**
>
> Then, as today, the Pope was the supreme head of the Catholic Church. He still resides in Rome, in the Vatican, the administrative and spiritual hub of the Church. Though some English people did make pilgrimages to Rome in the Middle Ages, it is unlikely that the Pardoner, given his hypocritical view of religion, would have made such a long and arduous trip.

CONTEXT

There is irony in the Host's claim that the Pardoner would try and get him to kiss 'thyn old breech' because one of the things pilgrims did when they worshipped at Canterbury was to kiss the hair breeches or under-garments that St Thomas wore. It may be that Chaucer is suggesting here that the less than pious Host is with the pilgrims more for the social outing than to worship at the martyr's shrine.

ambiguously 'I wol no lenger pleye/ with thee' (682–3), suggesting that his recent outburst might have been only intended as a joke or piece of fun, not genuine anger. The Knight suggests simply to the Pardoner that he should accept that 'it is right ynough/ … [to] be glad and myrie of cheere' (676–7), even if the pilgrims' laughter is at his expense. Order being restored through the amiable but authoritative figure of the noble Knight, the pilgrims ride on.

GLOSSARY

610	traitours homicide	betraying murderer
619	And ware yow fro	and beware of
620	alle warice	will heal all
621	nobles or sterlinges	gold coins worth one third of a pound, and silver pennies
627	I yow assoille	I absolve you
628	as clene and eek as cleer	as clean and as clear
630	oure soules leche	heal our souls
638	and han myn absolucion	and have my absolution
641	as ye wende	as you travel
646	suffisant	competent
649	Paraventure	perhaps
658	everychon	everyone
659	Unbokele	unbuckle, undo
661	so theech	so may I prosper
664	thy fundement depeint	stained by your bottom
667	seintuarie	a casket or ornamental box to hold relics
668	Lat kutte hem of	Let me cut them off
671	So wrooth he was	he was so angry

EXTENDED COMMENTARIES

Text 1 – *The Pardoner's Prologue*, lines 43–90

Chaucer uses this passage to introduce the voice and character of the Pardoner. He is one of the most complex and remarkable figures in the whole of *The Canterbury Tales*. Through an extended confession of his life as a fraudster and his skilful delivery of a 'demonstration **sermon**', he unashamedly reveals his contempt for other people's religious beliefs. He places himself at the centre of his Tale, while the actual moral story he tells to entertain the pilgrims is a small part of his whole Prologue and Tale.

The voice of the Pardoner is strong and confident from the start of the Prologue. This is reinforced by the strong, simple end rhymes of the opening couplets: 'preche/speche, belle/telle' (44–7). It is important that the sound of the Pardoner's voice is conveyed, not just the meaning of his words. We can imagine that the Pardoner, as a professional public speaker, has been looking forward to his turn to tell a story and is beginning it with gusto. He has waited a long time: most orderings of *The Canterbury Tales* place his Tale thirteenth or fifteenth, approximately halfway through the whole collection.

The Pardoner runs through the process by which he begins his preaching. He appears proud of his deceptions. Again the rhymes are clear and strong, suggesting a man clearly laying out the way he works: 'come/um', 'clerk/werk', 'shewe/few', for example. The pace is rapid, there is no digression into any explanation of personal motives, nor into **allusions** or references. This passage shows Chaucer at his most efficient and clear as a narrative writer, covering a lot of information in neatly rhymed **iambic pentameter** couplets. This measure of verse is also known as the heroic couplet and is the key structural feature of most of the writing Chaucer did in his later life (after 1386).

From line 51 on the air of professional authority that the Pardoner gives himself (falsely as it turns out) begins to show. He describes how he presents his official warrants and letters of authority to counter any

CONTEXT

Chaucer wrote over 16,000 lines of **heroic couplets** (or over 8,000 rhymed couplets). He is generally regarded as the writer who developed the form in English, probably using it first in his poem *Compleynte to Pitee* (circa 1372).

TEXT 1 – *THE PARDONER'S TALE*, LINES 43–90 continued

There is a long, varied and often gruesome tradition of miraculous bones in Christian stories. Perhaps the best-known is that of the prophet Elisha whose skeleton was exposed when his corpse was dug up (for some unclear reason). Another body thrown into the re-opened grave returned to life because of contact with Elisha's holy bones. Elisha appears sporadically through I Kings in the Old Testament.

objections to him from 'preest ne clerk' (53). He claims he has 'Bulles' from popes (note the plural), which are documents too powerful and rare for a mere travelling pardoner reasonably to be expected to have been granted. These boastful words indicate the self-importance and high self-regard that increasingly dominates the Pardoner's demonstration **sermon**. It is this same blind self-regard that causes his 'downfall' at the hands of the Host at the end of the Tale.

The focus on relics that might be of use to an agrarian community shows that the Pardoner both understands the needs of his target audience and that Chaucer is providing the less educated listeners to his Tales with examples they can easily understand. A bone that confers veterinary healing properties to animals' drinking water and a mitten used for casting seed in hand-sowing that will increase the crop's yield would obviously be desirable items for people used to a difficult agricultural life. Focusing on practical aspects of daily life also provides a contrast to the ideas explored in the demonstration sermon and the **moral tale** that form the bulk of the Pardoner's subject matter.

This whole passage is about establishing the Pardoner's remarkable character. In a story which has deception as one of its key themes, the fact that the Pardoner is a walking embodiment of it needs to be subtly but forcefully introduced. Chaucer does not reveal the depths of the Pardoner's deceits all at once: rather the Pardoner himself gradually exposes them in his confession. Chaucer gives us hints of what depths of hypocrisy are to be revealed by the Pardoner's claim (80) that, as well as curing sick animals, the same water that is miraculously changed by the bone can also be used by adulterous wives to cure husbands of jealousy. (For more on the relics in this section, see **Detailed summary,** *The Pardoner's Prologue*, lines 1–91).

TEXT 2 – *THE PARDONER'S TALE*, LINES 263–302

This passage is the second time that the Pardoner has spoken against the sin of drunkenness. His focus on this particular sin of indulgence is partly due to the fact that the Flemish young men he has introduced are drinkers, and perhaps partly because drinking to excess was a sin that he could be sure many of the pilgrims would be likely to fall prey to. It was one that, in a sense, ordinary people could hope to afford. This is in contrast to a sin like 'sloth' for example, which in a society where not to work to the point of exhaustion often meant economic ruin for most people was an unattainable luxury as well as a sin. The pilgrims may be listening to this sitting in a roadside inn. If we imagine the Pardoner gradually becoming more passionate as he progresses through his extensive attacks on various sins, we can regard him as in full-volume rhetorical flow here. Yet his sermon, his attack on drinking, is strangely compromised in terms of dramatic drive by his curious digression into the wine trade (see **Detailed Summaries:** *The Pardoner's Tale*, lines 263–302).

Despite the air of digression, Chaucer may have deliberately included this information to amuse his readers. The point of mentioning towns that produce good wine, those who produce bad and the fact that the drunk at home in 'Chepe' (278) in London will think himself in Spain where the wine comes from, is two-fold. Firstly wine merchants can adulterate wine (adding poor wine to good and selling the result as good) to increase their profits, another example of the theme of deception; and secondly, that drinking to excess befuddles the drinker.

Chaucer's use of contemporary details of the London wine importing trade (his father was a wine merchant) would have appealed to his audience and reflects a key and unique element of Chaucer's writing. There was no tradition of written popular fiction in medieval England. All texts had to be handwritten, and such exhaustive labour was generally reserved for treatise on moral, theological or political subjects. 'Stories', especially those designed to appeal to ordinary people, were the preserve of the oral tradition, which was principally delivered by travelling minstrels. Chaucer bridged the world of non-fiction texts (of which he wrote several), **courtly** poetry and (with *The Canterbury Tales*) popular stories that had the humour, energy and realism to appeal to a wide audience. His London audience especially would have smiled appreciatively at the mention of a trade they knew about and of streets, such as 'Fisshstrete' and 'Chepe' (278) which they might have walked down.

CHECK THE BOOK

A good example of a novelist using digressions to add variety to his narrative can be found in *Moby Dick* (1851) a story of a whaling ship's captain's obsession with killing the eponymous whale. The author, Herman Melville (1819–91), includes long factual passages about the whaling industry to paint a vivid picture of the world in which the story is set. *Moby Dick* is regarded as one of the greatest American novels of the nineteenth century.

CONTEXT

In Chaucer's time, and for many centuries afterwards, Cheapside was a busy market area of London, close to the docks and wharves of the River Thames where imported goods such as wine were landed from ships.

The Pardoner has a number of lines in this section that state simple good moral principles. These are apparently heartfelt: the assumption he wants a congregation to make is that he abides by what he so clearly states. Of course we know he is guilty of indulging in the pleasures of eating and drinking and that this is just another aspect of his deception. There are such statements at intervals throughout the demonstration **sermon**, but they are particularly noticeable here. 'In whom that drinke hath dominacioun /He kan no conseil kepe' (274–5) and 'A capitain sholde live in sobrenesse' (296) are two striking example of clear moral observation and comment.

TEXT 3 – *THE PARDONER'S TALE*, LINES 520–64

This dramatically crucial and fast-moving section of the Tale splits the action between two events and locations. First we see the two young men who are left behind plotting a murder while guarding the treasure they have just discovered. Then we move to the third one of the group who is running to town to get supplies for their vigil, and through his conversation with himself (his inner voice) we discover what he is fatally tempted to do. This passage reveals the depths to which the sinners will sink; that they will turn on one another. It shows that the sin of avarice has no limits and that there is no honour among thieves.

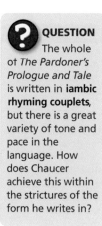

QUESTION
The whole of *The Pardoner's Prologue and Tale* is written in **iambic rhyming couplets,** but there is a great variety of tone and pace in the language. How does Chaucer achieve this within the strictures of the form he writes in?

Chaucer makes good use of quoted direct speech throughout the passage. We hear exactly how one man persuades the other into plotting murder and this is much more immediate and urgent than reported speech. As ever, the simple pattern of rhyming couplets drives the narrative forward, especially when spoken aloud.

The use of questions further engages the reader/ listener with the story. At line 529 the man who suggests the murder of their friend says that if he could see a way to make the division of the gold go only two ways, 'Hadde I nat doon a freendes torn to thee?' – 'would I not be doing you a good turn?' Being wicked, they are both morally blind to the reverse of this – are they not doing a bad turn to the one it is suggested they kill? But the sin of avarice has blinded them to logic as well as loyalty.

The man to whom the plot is put needs little persuasion. He seems instantly more concerned with how they could effect a two (rather than three) way division of the treasure. The plan to start a mock fight when the third returns, and then for them both to stab him, is presented and easily agreed. Temptation hovers over this passage: the two conspirators imagine how they will spend their enlarged shares, 'Thanne may we bothe oure lustes all fulfille' (547).

Meanwhile the third young man is running alone to town. He too is tempted to enlarge his share of the treasure. The Pardoner uses the striking image of the beauty of the coins rolling up and down in his heart to suggest how the temptation is actually moving within him (552–3). Then the 'feend', the fiend or devil (558), enters his thoughts, and he resolves to kill his waiting friends. Not only does he plan this murder, but he is clear that, just like those he plans to kill, he will never repent it.

The whole of this passage is focused to dramatic purpose and rapid narrative drive. There are no digressions or **allusions**. Evil intentions dominate everyone. None of the three men has for a moment any pang of conscience about what they are planning. The Pardoner promised a **moral tale**, so the pilgrims listening know the three men are being set up ready to be mortally punished for their intended crimes – but it is not yet clear how they will be brought down. The end of this passage is a moment of high expectation for the pilgrims.

CONTEXT
In line 553 one of the young men refers to 'florins newe and brighte'. A florin was the name for coins of different values in a number of different currencies. In England it was a coin worth six shillings in pre-decimal currency (30 pence) that was minted only in 1344.

PART THREE

CRITICAL APPROACHES

CHARACTERISATION

CONTEXT
Another well known character from *The Canterbury Tales*, the openly sensual Wife of Bath, is good example of a character drawn from estate satire. Her character is based largely on the stereotypical image of domineering wives popular in **misogynist** literature dealing with the imagined miseries of marriage.

We cannot judge the characters Chaucer creates in *The Pardoner's Tale* by the same standards we would employ to assess protagonists in a modern work of fiction. In the Middle Ages the works of fiction that existed often treated characters as **allegorical** figures: they **personified** ideas such as 'Virtue' or 'Innocence'. Death personified was a major figure of this general type. These were symbolic figures, not intended to represent complex fictional human characters. Other types were derived from folk traditions or classical tales. These were often defined almost entirely by their role in a story: the revenger, the hero, the honest man, the corrupt official, for example. Other characters were the 'stock' figures from a popular type of story known as **estate satires**. These featured variations of a standard and recognised cast defined by their employment and social standing. The **genre** was **satirical** insofar as these characters always embodied failings, and estate satires were built around these.

The degree to which Chaucer depicted recognisable everyday people was unique in the literature of the Middle Ages. The vividness of his characters, especially their voices when they speak directly within the poetry of *The Canterbury Tales*, is often regarded as the work's most enduring quality. Chaucer is more than a satirist, although some of the characters in *The Canterbury Tales*, for example the Friar who loves the good life more than prayer, could be drawn from estate satires. His stories contain or imply moral dimensions, but again the range and complexity of his characterisation shows that he is much more than a moralist using allegorical figures to expound moral themes. One of Chaucer's greatest achievements is his range of characters in *The Canterbury Tales*. They show him to be a brilliant and genial observer of humanity in all its goodness and badness, glory and folly.

THE PARDONER

There is only one figure that we would regard as a fully-developed character in *The Pardoner's Tale:* the eponymous Pardoner himself. We learn a great deal about him, mostly from his own 'confessions' but also from Chaucer, standing back as an observer. He does this chiefly through his description of the Pardoner in *The General Prologue*. We also gain some understanding of the Pardoner from remarks made to him by other pilgrims. Critics regard the Pardoner as the most complex and fully realised character in all of *The Canterbury Tales* (see **Part Four: Critical perspectives**).

The voice of the Pardoner – loud, upbeat, **rhetorically** confident and unabashed – sings out from every line of his Tale. He is sure of everything he says and convinced that he has the skill to hold an audience with his personal confession, **sermonising** and storytelling. He is confident that he will always create the effect upon them that he intends (which is why he is so shocked at the Host's outburst at the end of the Tale).

The Pardoner explains to the pilgrims with brazen honesty what he does and why. He cheats simple country parsons and their congregations because he wants their money to fund a comfortable life for himself. No detailed motivation for this is provided, as we might expect from a character in a modern novel. A modern novelist might for example reveal that the Pardoner grew up in poverty next to a cathedral where clergymen lived lives of plenty and this made him angry and determined to revenge himself on religion. Background information like this might even make us feel sympathy for the Pardoner. But such detail does not fit with either the cultural context of *The Canterbury Tales* or the Pardoner's character – he does not feel the need to justify himself to the pilgrims. In contrast to medieval verse narratives and dramas, revenge tragedies, a genre of dramatic writing that reached its height in the Elizabethan theatre, operated on the notion of a wrong needing to be righted. Although these plays were written two centuries after Chaucer in a more sophisticated literary context, their protagonists were generally driven by much simpler motives than any we could imagine for the complex character of the Pardoner.

CHECK THE BOOK

Dramatist Cyril Tourneur (also spelt Turnour or Turner, 1575–1626) is known to have created two **revenge tragedies**, the best known of which, *The Revenger's Tragedy* (1607), is a very good example of the **genre**. Violent and gloomy, it deals with the revenge of Vendice for the murder of his mistress by a morally degenerate duke.

One of the remarkable achievements of *The Canterbury Tales* is that Chaucer broke with many literary conventions. For example, in the literature of the Middle Ages the link between good deeds and reward, and bad deeds and punishment, was expected. To suggest that good deeds could go unrewarded or villainy go unpunished broke both artistic and moral codes. Yet the Pardoner is a rogue who apparently gets away with his villainy, and, even more shocking, revels in what he does. Added to the novelty and shock of this is the fact that many of the pilgrims, and Chaucer's readers, would have seen this reflected in what happened in reality. Corrupt pardoners were ill-regarded figures in the popular imagination in the Middle Ages (see **Reading** *The Pardoner's Tale*).

If we explore the cultural context of *The Pardoner's Tale* a little more deeply we might say that Chaucer, in creating such a corrupt character, is implying criticism of the Church. He is suggesting that the Church, through its dominance of social and spiritual life, creates characters like the Pardoner and that such characters inevitably lack the self-will, even the self-awareness, to act in any different way. The notion of self-determination, of people being able to control their destiny through changing their personality, was not part of the mind set of Middle Ages. 'Self-fashioning' or self-determination was an idea that was created in the Renaissance.

It is a mistake to look for any characters that have 'internal lives', who reveal their thoughts and feelings beyond simple motives and emotions, in a work written as early as *The Canterbury Tales*. Critics often identify Shakespeare's Hamlet as the first character to be written with a real internal life, in a play written two hundred years after Chaucer's death. Shakespeare uses many lines of verse to explore, analyse and query Hamlet's thoughts and emotions. He is a fully created character full of human ambiguities, doubts, moods and contradictions. Characters were not written like this in Chaucer's time. They were more one-dimensional, usually driven by one motive within a story, like the young men in *The Pardoner's Tale* who are almost automatically compelled by their insatiable need to sin. The complex and realistically human idea of ambiguity in a fictional character was not a feature of medieval creative thinking. The fact that the Pardoner explains in such detail what he does, how he appears to be one thing but is really another, is a remarkable feat of invention by Chaucer.

CONTEXT

The Renaissance was a great flowering of art and original individual thought that began in Italy at the end of the Middle Ages, just overlapping the last years of Chaucer's life. It spread across Europe in the fifteenth century and reached its peak, the High Renaissance, in the early sixteenth century. Key to its many elements was the exploration of the individual and human as independent from God.

Much of what the Pardoner reveals about himself is covered in the **Detailed summaries** and **Extended commentaries**. His 'confession' of his true self is completely bound up with the Tale he actually tells and the narrative frame he sets it within. It is sufficient here to remind ourselves that he is quite happy to confess that he is a hypocrite, constantly committing the very sin of greed that he preaches against. He says plainly 'I preche nothing but for coveitise' (147). Neither Chaucer the author nor any of the pilgrims makes any direct criticism of what the Pardoner does, possibly because at the time Chaucer was writing the system of pardoners was widely regarded as totally corrupt. True, the Host is furious with the Pardoner at the end of the Tale, but this is a personal altercation. We imagine that if he had not been singled out as a sinner in special need of a pardon, the Host would have been as quiet as everyone else at the end of the Tale.

In addition to narrating his own Tale, the Pardoner also makes a brief but significant appearance in *The Wife of Bath's Prologue*. (Like *The Pardoner's Tale*, *The Wife of Bath's Tale* is one of the best-known stories from the whole work.) In most versions of *The Canterbury Tales*, this Tale follows directly after the Pardoner's. We might imagine the Pardoner still thinking about how the pilgrims laughed at him when he was insulted by the Host. What he says in *The Wife of Bath's Prologue*, about a hundred and fifty lines after the row with the Host, might be motivated by the effect he has just had on the pilgrims and their reactions to his Tale. He wants to be part of the group again.

 CHECK THE BOOK

In *Chaucer and his Poetry* (Harvard University Press, 1915) George Kittredge looks at the tellers of the Tales as dramatic characters and links the stories they tell to their personalities.

The Pardoner interrupts the Wife of Bath's long *Prologue* in which she is talking about marriage and how she seeks to have the power within it. He praises her 'preaching' (like a professional public speaker approving the efforts of an amateur) and says that he was about to take a wife, but, hearing what she has to say, he thinks he will not marry this year. This revelation certainly bears on Chaucer's observation in *The General Prologue* that the Pardoner might be a eunuch or a woman in disguise. It also impacts on suggestions made by some critics that the pilgrims think the Pardoner is homosexual because of his physical appearance and strange costume.

CHECK THE BOOK

In the *Prologue to the Miller's Tale* – a very bawdy, crude story – Chaucer, through the character of the Host, intervenes to ask readers to be tolerant. He suggests that such a varied collection of Tales must contain something for everyone and that more sensitive readers should perhaps find a different story.

We may think that if the pilgrims read the Pardoner's appearance in this way, this might add another layer to the disdain they feel towards him. However, in medieval times people thought more about individual sexual acts and relationships than an individual's sexual identity, and so Chaucer's pilgrims might be more tolerant of the Pardoner's sexuality than we might imagine. The modern reader, however, is entitled to wonder whether the Pardoner is telling the truth about his plan to marry in *The Wife of Bath's Prologue*, or whether is he trying to persuade the pilgrims that he is as heterosexual as the bluff and energetic Host with whom he has just argued. There is no way to tell, but it is a measure of Chaucer's skill as a writer controlling the whole structure of his work, that he slips in this curious comment from the Pardoner after he has so extensively revealed his character in his Tale.

One question we can't answer about the Pardoner is whether he actually believes in God. If he does, then his desire for a good life for himself is stronger than his religious convictions. If he doesn't, then he is doubly hypocritical, pretending to hold a belief he doesn't subscribe to in order to defraud those who do. There is no evidence in the text to argue this issue either way. However, if we consider the Pardoner as a character of his time, we might conclude that it would be very remarkable indeed if he were an agnostic or an atheist. More likely he believes in a Christian god in some basic way, but not in the authority of his Church as an organisation on earth (for more on this subject, see **Themes: Religion**).

THE THREE YOUNG MEN

The three young men in the Tale are 'types' rather than fully realised characters with definite identities. They exist primarily to play their parts in the story. They are symbolic habitual sinners. We do not learn anything about their lives except that they spend their days wickedly: eating and drinking to excess, 'over hir might' (182) 'more than they could hold', gambling, cursing and blaspheming. It is sufficient to know that these men represent an entire way of life for *The Pardoner's Tale* to work dramatically for the pilgrims.

The trio are differentiated from one another by odd lines, but as they are never named it is not possible for us to develop a picture of, for example 'the proudeste of thise riotoures' (430); nor do we know if this proud one is the same as 'the yonseste' (551) who draws the straw that sends him into town for supplies. When they speak we cannot identify their separate voices. This is deliberate; the implication being that sin overrides personality. They might be differentiated by having personal predilections for specific sins (one a drinker, one a glutton, one committed to sexual excess, for example) but this is not necessary for the Tale to work. Chaucer doesn't complicate our knowledge of them or slow the narrative down by revealing this.

Their speech reveals their common sinful character. The one who speaks to the old man is aggressive and threatening. The two left with the treasure show themselves to be equally quick to plot to murder their supposed friend: specifically they twist the concept of friendship to create a pact against their absent friend. The purpose of these exchanges is not to develop their characters but simply to show that they are aggressive and duplicitous. They do not appear to be very intelligent or full of insight. They take things that happen at face value. They never consider that there might be a link between the old man's directions and the appearance of the treasure. Indeed the Pardoner does not give them any redeeming features (except that we might see their plan to kill Death as intended to be some sort honourable revenge for Death killing their friend), nor suggest any hint of justification or excuse for their habitually immoral way of life. They are sinners and he needs to make them contemptible in all respects so that their deaths by the own hands are even more deserved and satisfying for the pilgrims. Although the Pardoner never says so, we feel that the three men have freely chosen their sinful way of life.

The degree to which the three young men are archetypes can be assessed by our reactions to their deaths. We do not feel sympathy, because they are all villains, or delight, because they each get what they deserve. We feel instead pleasure in the neat and striking conclusion of a plot. For the Pardoner, and for Chaucer's construction of his great work, it is the story and its message that is important, not any particular human outcomes for the characters who act it out. We know nothing about the families of the three men, for example, or what happens after their deaths.

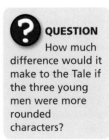

QUESTION
How much difference would it make to the Tale if the three young men were more rounded characters?

**CHECK
THE POEM**

Another example of a mysterious (and elderly) figure casting a long shadow into a story is the ancient mariner in the long narrative poem *The Rime of the Ancient Mariner* by Samuel Taylor Coleridge (1772–1834). The tragic mariner waylays a guest on his way to a wedding party and beguiles him with his haunting story.

THE OLD MAN

The old man is the first and only person the three men meet, 'Whan they han goon nat fully half a mile' (425). We learn that he is old and 'povre' – poor – and that he greets them 'ful mekely' (427–8). Throughout his appearance, he speaks simply and humbly but with wisdom tinged with an air of mystery and melancholy.

The old man is the only character, apart from the three young men, who speaks for any length or to any purpose in the Tale. He is a mysterious figure and has been the subject of much critical speculation. Is he in league with Death, or Death himself in disguise? The Tale of which he is so vital a part is Chaucer's version of a folk story that had existed in different forms for centuries. In neither these nor Chaucer's version is it clear exactly who the man is.

This enigmatic old man does have human dimensions and qualities, however, and these are revealed in his speeches between lines 429–81. He greets the three men politely when they first meet. They, in return, suggest he has lived too long to be so old (line 433). This is almost a threat, certainly an insult, but the old man appears not be nervous or taken aback. As their meeting progresses we sense what the trio appear not to notice: that for a frail old man accosted by three probably drunk and certainly aggressive young men, he is in no way afraid of anything they say. This suggests to us that he may have hidden powers that lend him a confidence the young men don't apparently see. If, for example, the old man is Death **personified**, then he has no need to fear them.

**CHECK
THE FILM**

The idea of Death as a grim figure wandering the earth claiming souls was used to great dramatic effect in Ingmar Bergman's film *The Seventh Seal* (1957) in which a knight plays chess with Death for his life.

If the three young men were less focused on their plan to murder the thief called Death, they might have paused to consider that much of what the old man says is rather odd. He has travelled as far as 'Inde' (India) looking for any young man who would swap his youth for the old man's age – not an attractive or likely exchange. The old man paints a pitiful picture of himself wandering about knocking on the earth, Mother Earth, asking to be taken in. He says, mysteriously and somewhat eerily, that now not even Death will take my life – 'Ne Deeth, allas, ne wol nat han my lyf' (441). This is suggesting that he has in some way become immortal, been singled out not to be allowed to die, perhaps by Death: or that he has become Death himself.

THE HOST

The 'Hooste' (1) or 'hoost' (678) is a lively and human figure in this otherwise quite dark and **gothic** Tale. He appears in *The Introduction to the Pardoner's Tale*, touched by the tragedy of the story they have just heard, *The Physician's Tale*. We might regard him as being easily moved to shows of sentimentality. He invites the Pardoner to tell a merry Tale to cheer everyone up. He calls the Pardoner 'thou beel ami' (32), a good friend. This is characteristic of the Host's good nature. It is his offer of a free dinner for the best Tale told on the journey that is underlying the whole idea of *The Canterbury Tales*. He makes this generous offer before they set out from his inn – 'and which of yow that…telleth in this cass/ Tales of best sentence and moost solaas,/ Shall have a soper at oure aller cost/ here in this place' (*The General Prologue*, 798–801).

The Host has a temper, though his outbursts are usually short-lived. He reveals this when he is invited to be the first to open his purse and buy a worthless pardon. The Host says he would like to pull the Pardoner's testicles off and enshrine them in a hog's turd! The Pardoner has suggested that the Host, of all the pilgrims, is 'moost envoluped in sinne' (656). The Host may have a temper, and work in a trade that could be seen as promoting drunkenness, but the overall impression we get from his appearances throughout the Tales is of a man who is both amiable and easily moved by the stories the pilgrims tell.

THE PILGRIMS

It would be fair to sum up the pilgrims' attitude towards the Pardoner as cool at best, confrontational (in the case of the Host) at worst. As ever in the Tales, they appear a fairly tolerant and accepting group of people. Given that they are on a pilgrimage (albeit not a very arduous one), they don't exhibit any adverse reaction to what they have heard from the Pardoner. It is hard to see how they feel towards the Pardoner because Chaucer does not generally include responses from individual pilgrims to various Tales. Apart from the Host, no one actually attacks the Pardoner for attempting to sell them pardons. Equally, no one offers any line of defence to support him doing what, in historical fact, most pardoners did. Prompted by the Host's outraged insults, they laugh at the Pardoner. The Knight

CHECK THE BOOK

The Pilgrim's Progress, published in 1687 by John Bunyan (1628–88), is a long narrative poem that treats the idea of pilgrimage in a totally **allegorical** manner. The pilgrim meets characters who symbolise spiritual and moral virtues or ills with names like Mr Worldly Wiseman and Giant Despair.

only intervenes (674) to separate the Host and the Pardoner for the general good of the company and to get their journey underway again, not to protect the Pardoner himself.

THEMES

DECEPTION

Deception is present on many levels in *The Pardoner's Tale*. The first element of deception, though it is in a sense an implied one within the whole idea of fiction, is that the Pardoner never says if the Tale he tells is true. (Of course, none of the other pilgrims claim their Tales are true either.) In a sense it doesn't matter as the pilgrims want a Tale with a moral theme, and he provides this in a vivid and engaging way. It doesn't matter if it never really occurred: it is to be enjoyed as a warning of the dangers of sinning, and as an example of what could happen to you if you transgress. It is a variation on a well-known folk tale, but many storytellers would introduce such a story, however formulaically, by suggesting that it was based on truth. The Pardoner doesn't feel the need to break the mythic timeless air of his story by suggesting it may have really happened.

The Pardoner's life is based on deceiving people into parting with their money. We learn nothing about him beyond his methods as a habitual fraudster and his enjoyment of the profits of his many deceptions. However, as his Tale is largely a confession to the other pilgrims of his cheating, he does not try to deceive them about his true nature. It could be said that this makes his whole Tale a great display of honesty. We are given no clue as to why the Pardoner is suddenly being so open. Does this suggest a desire on his part to join the group as fully and honestly as he can? There is no evidence that this is the case. When at the end of the Tale he tries to sell them the very relics and pardons he has already told them are worthless, it is possible that he is so lost in what he is doing that he is unaware of the extent of his deception, and in this is unthinkingly deceiving himself.

Three clear strands of deception run through the plot of the Tale. The three men deceive themselves into believing they can kill the thief called Death. They are apparently deceived by the old man into going to where the gold awaits them – either because the old man is Death in disguise or because he is some supernatural agent in league with Death. Finally, they bring about their own deaths by two acts of deception against each other.

A further level of deception is contained in the way Chaucer treats the identity of the Pardoner. His description in *The General Prologue* picks out his odd appearance, and notes his 'small voice' and hairless chin. Chaucer suggests the Pardoner may be a eunuch. Some critics have said that maybe he is a woman dressed as a man. James Winny in his introduction to the Cambridge University Press edition of *The General Prologue* (1978) does not go so far as to suggest the Pardoner is female but emphasises his lack of male virility. He refers to the Pardoner as 'emasculated' and attempting 'an imposture of being a virile and attractively wild young man' (pages 39–40). It is possible that from the very moment the Pardoner appears he attempts to deceive the pilgrims about his sexual identity.

Deception was a powerful and emotive theme for Chaucer's readers. In the Middle Ages, most people had far less recourse to law than we do. Being cheated by another person was a constant fear. In addition, most people believed in the idea that the Devil was abroad in the world, able to change his appearance in order to cause harm. If you were not careful, if you neglected your prayers, you could be deceived by him into some sort of unholy trap. He would take your possessions or your life and then even your soul. People were generally suspicious of anything and anyone they did not know. It was the superstitious fear of people who appeared different, or were outsiders in some way, that led to so many accusations of witchcraft throughout the Middle Ages. The pilgrims would have been gripped by a Tale that has deception as one of its themes and its main dramatic drive.

CHECK THE NET

For information on the culture of the Middle Ages, go to **http://medieval. etrusia.co.uk**

CORRUPTION

There is a strong sense of physical corruption, of decay, disfigurement and decline, throughout *The Pardoner's Tale*, especially in the demonstration **sermon**. 'O dronke man, disfigured is thy face' (265) is a blunt picture of a drunkard's ravaged face, while the image of cooks who 'Out of the harde bones knokke they/ The mary, for they caste noght awey' (254–6) turns the art of frugal cooking into something crude and gross. Decay casts a shadow throughout *The Pardoner's Prologue* and *Tale*. The image of the 'povereste widwe in a village,/ al sholde hir children sterve for famine' (164–5) after she has been relieved of her money by the Pardoner is bleak and cruel. The plague-ravaged village described by the taverner as the place where Death can be found, 'I trowe his habitacioun be there' (403), is a darkly **gothic** image.

Sins like drunkenness and gluttony result in physical disfigurement such as bloating and foul breath. Many of the relics the Pardoner mentions are physically unpleasant (more so to us than Chaucer's contemporaries). They are the residue of physical decay, bones and rags. Chaucer, through the Pardoner, focuses again and again back to the idea that while all things will decline and rot away, wickedness accelerates the process. Powerful images of physical decay occur throughout the whole text.

This focus on physical decay reflects the moral and spiritual corruption of the Pardoner. To the extent that we see things through his eyes, it could be said that he sees the physical corruption in the world not merely as useful images to convince a congregation of the effects of sin, but because, being morally corrupt himself, he cannot help himself seeing the inevitable physical rot and decay in everything around him. We might link this to the notion that the Pardoner is a victim of his own habitual deceptions. If he is so contemptuous of the world, how can he ever rejoice in anything within it, except in a gleefully malignant sort of way? Yet he tries to present himself as a man who spends the money he extorts on licentious and extravagant 'good living' – 'I wol drinke licour of the vine, / and have a joly wenche in every toun' (166–7). This sort of life suggests a jolly, gregarious personality, but the Pardoner is far too dark, too mired in sin, to be convincingly described in such a way.

This focus on physical corruption through powerful visual images increases the gothic mood of the Prologue and Tale. As in the most extreme gothic literature there is a pervading sense of darkness, of things unpleasant and macabre. Nowhere in the Prologue and Tale is

 CHECK THE NET

To see how central veneration of relics was to Christians in the Middle Ages, read *On Saints and Their Relics* by Guibert of Nogent (1053–1124). He was the abbot of a traditional Benedictine monastery. A version of the text can be read online at **http://www.fordham.edu** – search for 'Nogent'.

there anything innocent or sunlit; nowhere is anything described which is without blemish. Even in *The General Prologue*, which is generally upbeat and almost practical in tone, the description of the Pardoner's appearance introduces a hint of something sinister and abnormal.

GLUTTONY AND DRUNKENNESS

These two sins may not always seem as dreadful to us as modern readers, and certainly not as serious as some of the other of the cardinal sins. Most of us live in a world of relative plenty where personal overindulgence generally brings negative consequences only upon the glutton or drunk and perhaps their family and dependents. However, the theological and moral view of these sins was different in Chaucer's time. Committing any kind of sin and being absolved of it, was a very important part of religious observance in the medieval Church. Resources to sustain human life were neither abundant nor consistently available so the glutton could be seen as insulting, if not directly contributing to, the plight of the starving. The sense of dislike the Pardoner can expect the pilgrims to have for the three young men who are such gluttons and drunks is much greater than we might expect.

Life for most people in England (and Europe) in the later Middle Ages was a struggle to survive. Wealth was held by a small elite of noble families gathered around the king. Most of the population were poor and lived in permanent fear of starvation. Europe suffered the Great Famine between 1315 and 1322. Crops failed for three consecutive summers (1315–17) and starvation was widespread until 1322. Chroniclers reported cannibalism (though historians debate how widespread this actually may have been). Infant mortality rates in England through the whole of the Middle Ages have been estimated at thirty per cent or more even in years without famine. In 1381, the Peasants Revolt led by Wat Tyler broke out in protest against taxes on poor labourers. The king, Richard II, promised reforms but broke all his promises. Disease was rampant, and the Black Death killed a third of the population of England in 1349. Living with this constant fear of disaster, it is no wonder so many people sought relief in drunkenness whenever they could, and would gorge themselves on food if a sudden supply became available. The pilgrims might show support for the

CHECK THE BOOK

The Ties That Bound: Peasant families in Medieval England, Barbara Hanawalt (Oxford University Press, 1986) is a very scholarly but vivid account of life for working people in the Middle Ages.

Pardoner in his condemnation of overindulgence, but it is interesting to imagine which of them – the Monk or the Franklin, perhaps – might commit sins of drunkenness and gluttony if given the chance to do so without censure.

The Pardoner begins his lengthy discourse on drunkenness and gluttony prompted by his description of the three men in his Tale, eating and drinking to excess (182). As befits a **sermon**, he makes references to the Bible to support his condemnation of the evil effects of drunkenness (199–205). By line 212 he has moved on to encompass gluttony in his tirade – 'O glotonye, ful of cursednesse!'. His claims for the evils of excessive eating are themselves excessive, as befits a showman demonstrating how to engage a congregation – 'Corrupt was al this world for glotonye' (218). At line 222 the Pardoner makes an unattributed reference (he says simply 'as I rede') to an unusual interpretation of the biblical story of the expulsion of Adam and Eve from paradise to support his claims for the evils of gluttony.

The Pardoner knows he will have a hard job convincing a probably hungry congregation of the evils of gluttony, and so uses graphic physical **imagery** of its effects to repel them. A drinker makes a 'privee' (toilet) of his throat (241), a glutton's belly is a stinking pod, 'fulfilled of dong (dung) and corrupcioun!' (249).

RELIGION AND DISSENT

Given the historical and cultural context of Chaucer's world, it is reasonable to assume that the Pardoner and the pilgrims, Chaucer himself and his audience, all believed in God in the sense of how he was construed and worshipped within the creed of the Catholic Church in the Middle Ages.

However, in Chaucer's lifetime – and especially in the period when he was writing *The Canterbury Tales* – there were the stirrings of serious theological objections to core elements of orthodox Church doctrine. The best known expression of this dissent in England, and the most dangerous from the Church's point of view, was made by John Wyclif (1320–84) who was condemned as a heretic for the claim he made in his treatise *De Dominio Devine* (1376). In this, he

CONTEXT
The Church's usual punishment for a heretic in the Middle Ages was burning alive at the stake but for reasons that are unknown Wyclif managed to avoid this fate. Wyclif and his followers made the first translations of the Bible into English: he personally translated the Gospels and probably the whole of the New Testament.

claimed that all authority was founded on grace, and that wicked kings, popes and priests therefore should not hold power. As a philosopher and a widely-read man, he would have moved in the same intellectual world as Chaucer. It is not known if they ever met, but it is almost certain that Chaucer would have read Wyclif's works. What is not certain is the degree to which Chaucer, having read many of the same books as Wyclif, might himself have held radical and dissenting views towards the Church. He does not appear as an author making comments in his own right anywhere in *The Canterbury Tales*. Nothing we know about Chaucer's life suggests he was a radical, yet he allows his characters in the *Tales* to voice strong criticism of churchmen who are motivated by unholy intentions: 'many a predicioun [preaching] comth ofte time of yvel entencioun' (121–2). Indeed, one could argue that the best defence the Pardoner could offer for his grand scheme of deception would be to confess a lack of faith in God and the Church as an institution. Chaucer, however, does not allow the Pardoner to go this far. It is probably safest to assume, therefore, that while Chaucer may make fun of aspects of the Catholic Church and its members throughout *The Canterbury Tales*, and does so most darkly in *The Pardoner's Tale*, all his fictional creations are, even at their most critical, operating within an acceptance of Christian religion, and of the necessary primacy of the basic rules and scriptures of the Church.

Religion and the rituals of religious observance are in fact crucial to the structure and meaning of *The Pardoner's Tale*. The Pardoner makes his corrupt living by abusing the religious beliefs and practice of congregations. He employs **allusions** to biblical stories and characters throughout his **sermon** to add weight to his words. He demonstrates biblical knowledge but misuses it. He sees sin as corrupting God's work, and the sin of blaspheming as being particularly evil because it directly abuses the name of Christ. He tells a **moral tale** that is not moral in the purely human, ethical sense that might be employed today. The three men die not because they are freely operating individuals who have flawed personal characters, but because they are sinners and through their sins fall prey to the 'law' set down in the Bible that 'the love of money is the root of all evil'.

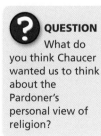

QUESTION
What do you think Chaucer wanted us to think about the Pardoner's personal view of religion?

**CHECK
THE BOOK**
*The Idea of The
Canterbury Tales*
(Donald R.
Howard,
University of
California Press,
1976) contains an
essay called 'The
Pardoner and the
Parson' which
compares the
hypocritical
Pardoner to the
honest Parson from
The Parson's Tale.
While the Pardoner
takes money from
the poor, the Parson
gives what little he
has to them.

AVARICE AND THE ABUSE OF POWER

Greed, the sin of avarice, is third in the list of the seven 'deadly' or cardinal sins. The Pardoner spends his whole life committing this sin, using the further (but not cardinal) sin of deception to satisfy his greed. He announces in the sixth line of his Prologue that his theme when preaching is always the same: '*Radix malorum est Cupiditas*' – 'The love of money is the root of all evil' – and he repeats this motto more than once during the Tale.

The Church in Chaucer's time had, in the creation of pardons and pardoners to gather money from sinners in return for absolution, established a very powerful source of income and a system rotten with corruption. Pardoners were regarded by most people as little more than confidence tricksters. More radical individuals also saw the Church as having great wealth, which they displayed in the treasures they kept in their churches and abbeys, while huge sections of the population of Europe constantly survived on the edge of starvation. While most of this popular dissent was at 'rumour' level, some individuals stood out and complained against the abuses. There was an undercurrent of dissent that is alluded to in comments found in correspondence of the time and mentioned by chroniclers, but only a few individuals stood out and complained publicly against the abuses. To stand up and openly challenge the Church, as Wyclif did, was a very bold step (see **Themes: Religion and dissent**).

The Pardoner has churchmen in his critical sights again when he is rather delightedly describing the false claims he makes for a 'holy bone', saying that water into which it has been immersed can be used to prevent jealousy. He suggests that a wife who makes her husband's broth from the water will prevent him becoming jealous even if 'al had she taken prestes two or three' (85) – even if she has had (sexually) two or three priests. Why should the Pardoner choose priests over any other sort of lover with which she might have multiple affairs? It is a small remark but suggests that the Pardoner (and Chaucer the author through the words of the Pardoner) has a very low view of the morals of churchmen. This passage also suggests that the Pardoner has an equally low opinion of women who are so ready to engage in such affairs, but this reflects the prevalent view of the period that saw women as morally weak and therefore in need of being guided by men. Everywhere else, however, the Pardoner seems contemptuous of individuals in the congregations he cheats regardless of their gender.

Within the cast of pilgrims in *The Canterbury Tales*, the Pardoner is the most clear and extreme example of someone with a religious title or position abusing his powers. He is also the character who gives most explanation of why he does this. Nonetheless, for a work that was written in a time of almost universal faith, there are a striking number of pilgrims who misuse the teachings and practices of the Church. Hubert the Friar is lecherous and avaricious. Less unpleasant but still sinful is the Monk, who loves good living above all else and prefers taverns to monastic life. The Summoner is a lay worker for the Church court service, and is portrayed as a physically repellent man, reflecting the repugnance that many people felt towards his work.

Against this group of men who do not live up to the high ideals of their calling, Chaucer balances other religious figures who do obey, honour or even exceed their vows. The Second Nun is a genuinely devout person, the humble Parson is poor because he gives his money to the needy. His actions are the very reverse of avarice.

DEATH

Death **personified**, a supernatural horror that walked the earth, was a real fear for many people in Chaucer's time. The idea of a thief called 'Death' stealing the souls of men may sound a little odd to a modern audience unused to seeing the world in such **metaphorical** terms, but this was a device that Chaucer's readers would have accepted as a necessary part of a highly moral story. 'The wages of sin is death' would be a phrase they would immediately understand, and the sinners in the Tale are paid almost instantly and by their own hands.

Despite his graphic descriptions of the horrible physical effects of gluttony and drunkenness, and his outraged tone, the Pardoner in his long tirade against sin from lines 199 to 373 only once mentions death as a direct consequence of committing a sin. He says as an aside that manslaughter (307) can result from gambling, when

> **CONTEXT**
>
> Churchmen were a much more prominent part of social life throughout most of the pre-twentieth century history of England than today. This is reflected in fictional portrayals of both good and bad figures. In Shakespeare's *Romeo and Juliet*, for example, Friar Lawrence is a crucial if misguided force for good in the plot, while in *Henry IV Part 2*, Archbishop Scroop is a self-aggrandising rebel who leads an army against the king.

> **CONTEXT**
>
> 'For the wages of sin is death, but the gift of God is eternal life through Jesus Christ our Lord' (Romans 6:23) is one of the best-known quotes from the Bible.

DEATH continued

 **CHECK
   THE BOOK**

The Divine Comedy
by the Italian poet
Dante Alighieri
(1265–1321), usually
know as Dante, is a
long narrative poem
which contains all
manner of deathly
horrors witnessed
by two characters
who travel through
the realms of hell
and purgatory.

people fight over the disputed result of a game or bet. The Pardoner
never directly mentions the outcome of the other sins he decries as
being fatal. Perhaps he assumes that everyone knows that decay
(about which he has lots to say) caused by wickedness will
inevitably lead to death. On the other hand, perhaps he is saving this
mortal outcome for the end of Tale itself.

STRUCTURE

The Pardoner's Tale is much more than a story told by one of the
pilgrims. It is important to understand how *The Pardoner's
Prologue* and the Tale itself fit together to make a whole, which is
created as much around the character of the Pardoner as the actual
Tale he tells. His Tale is actually quite short, only 323 lines out of
the Tale's total of 503. So how are the Prologue and the rest of the
Tale structured?

CONFESSION, SERMON AND MORAL TALE

The Pardoner uses the Prologue to 'confess'. For Chaucer's Catholic
audience, confession was an important religious practice (as it is for
many Catholics today), taking place in church and involving the
confession of recently committed sins. The Pardoner's is a very
different type of confession for it is without any of the shame or guilt
that such a term would conjure up for the pilgrims; he tells them that
he sells fake holy relics and pardons for money and feels no shame in
doing so. He uses the money he extracts from congregations to live a
comfortable life and expresses no desire to repent. Chaucer uses the
Prologue and some of the Tale itself to explore the nature of the
Pardoner and his particular style of confession.

The Pardoner's Prologue divides into two sections. From the
opening, line 43, to line 136, the Pardoner describes in a boastful,
almost gleeful, way how well he 'performs' as a preacher and what
fake relics he offers for sale to congregations. He quotes at length
the things he says to encourage the pious to come up and give him
money. This is the first part of his confession, where he explains the
techniques he uses to achieve his deceptions.

The second section of the Prologue begins at line 137 and from here to the end the Pardoner focuses on the second, more shocking, element of his confession. He makes his purpose in preaching plain: that everything he does is for his own gain. He concludes his Prologue by revealing the dark depths of his greed, then 'redeems' the moment by reminding the pilgrims of his skills as a public speaker – 'For though myself be a ful vicious man, / A moral Tale yet I yow telle kan' (173–4).

The Pardoner then begins his Tale, but after introducing his three riotous characters he breaks off and gives what is effectively a lengthy **sermon** on the nature of the sins he says they habitually commit. Again, he is demonstrating his sermonising skills to the pilgrims, drawing on another religious practice, this time of a sermon – or a speech with a strong moral message. He shows that he can speak powerfully and at length against a range of sins. He illustrates how he employs rhetorical techniques, demonstrates personal passion and fervour, and balances this with detailed references and **allusions** to biblical and other sources to endorse his condemnations. The sin of pride colours his delivery, making him keen to show just how effective he is at preaching to deceive.

This sudden digression, from the Tale to sermonising, can be read as a device to create anticipation among his listeners. It is the forerunner of the stand-up comedian's knack of introducing a story, then digressing off at a tangent. Hoping that the act is cleverly constructed, we assume that the story which has been suspended must be so good that we enjoy the digression in the knowledge that when the comedian returns to the original story, it will be worth the wait. The Pardoner, a practised public speaker, is using the structure of his Tale to create the same anticipation among the pilgrims.

It is not until line 374 ('But, sires, now wol I telle forth my tale'), almost two hundred lines on from when he broke off his account of the three sinners, that he returns to his Tale. This is a short and brilliantly focused moral story illustrating the claim that money is the root of all evil. As well as an entertainment for the pilgrims, it is

CHECK THE NET

For a wide range of examples of great **rhetorical** public speaking from the twentieth century, go to **www.guardian.co.uk** where you can read (and in some cases hear) speeches by Winston Churchill, Nelson Mandela, Martin Luther King and others. Enter 'great speeches' into the search box.

CONFESSION, SERMON AND MORAL TALE continued

CHECK THE BOOK

The 'whisky priest', the protagonist in the novel *The Power and the Glory*, (Graham Greene, 1940) is another ordained character who habitually commits the sins he is supposed to preach against.

a further example of how the Pardoner performs as a preacher – for this is the very Tale he tells congregations to prepare them for his 'sales pitch' for his holy relics. Indeed, the Tale concludes with a section in which the Pardoner swaps from being a storyteller to a salesman and tries to sell his worthless pardons to the pilgrims.

The Pardoner's Prologue and *The Pardoner's Tale* form one narrative unit centred round the character of the Pardoner. If you can grasp this overall structure, you will see how they fit together to present a highly effective **moral tale** and reveal much about the Pardoner as a character within the group of pilgrims.

NARRATIVE TECHNIQUES

CHAUCER'S AUTHORIAL POSITION

The authorial position of Chaucer within his own fiction is interesting. It is useful to have an understanding of this to see how *The Pardoner's Tale* works. *The Canterbury Tales* contains characters who speak to one another sporadically between stories in as natural a way as the poetic form allows. The Host is the most prominent and consistent of these voices. Most characters also become tellers of fictions within the bigger fiction of *The Canterbury Tales*. They are therefore characters telling stories about other characters that they create within their Tales. Often, like the Pardoner, they repeat directly what these characters say. Chaucer creates the clear voice of the Pardoner himself (arrogant and confident) who, as well as telling his whole Tale to the pilgrims, has long sections where he is quoting to them what he says to congregations. Then, in his Tale, he speaks as other characters: principally the young men and the old man. It is this range of voices that gives *The Canterbury Tales* its vitality and variety: it is also what hides the voice of Chaucer himself from us.

The very structure of *The Canterbury Tales* mitigates against a clear single authorial voice of the kind that, for example, modern novelists with a highly developed and recognisable literary style might bring to the story they are writing. Chaucer never intended us to hear 'his' voice. *The Canterbury Tales* are more like a work of drama which consists entirely of dialogue to be spoken by characters/actors, than a novel or narrative where authors create a prose style in which to tell their story, with more or less direct speech from characters as they wish. One of the great pleasures of *The Canterbury Tales* is hearing these 'ordinary' voices (especially of the characters speaking to one another between Tales) from the Middle Ages. Of course they are fictitious, for there never was such a group of pilgrims, though there must have been many who were very much like them. It is also important to remember that Chaucer sets himself within his own drama – one of the pilgrims/characters is the author himself, or a version of himself that Chaucer creates to be part of the company. He is a very minor figure in the work and at times almost hidden within it.

QUESTION
To what extent does Chaucer reveal himself through the characters he creates, and in the case of the Pardoner, what might he be revealing of his own ideas and opinions?

This Chaucer, the character, is an unassuming man. He always seems on the edge of things and is not a particularly confident or competent storyteller. Yet he embodies perfectly the overall tone of the work: of humanity, amiability and good nature. This is set up throughout *The General Prologue*, where we get the sense of a man keen to meet all his fellow pilgrims and to undertake the journey to Canterbury. As James Whiny says in his introduction to *The General Prologue* (Cambridge University Press, 1978), '*The Canterbury Tales* gives a modern reader the strongest sense of contact with the life and manners of fourteenth century England.' The character of Chaucer is our guide into this world (just as the amiable Host is the pilgrims guide along the road). We sense he will be happy to trot along with everyone and listen to their Tales, which is indeed the purpose Chaucer intends his character to fulfil, a neutral presence to make our reading of the Tales more enjoyable.

Chaucer's character seems pleased with the world. In the first lines (1–9) of the *General Prologue* he describes how April's showers are 'sweet (1), 'Zephirus' the warm west wind is a 'sweet breath' (5) and the 'smale fowles maken melodie'. (9). Chaucer seems to be contently saying, as another poet will put it several centuries later, 'God's in his heaven, all's right with the world'.

The Chaucer character we meet at the Tabard Inn seems far removed from the real Chaucer, the brilliant storyteller and successful public servant. Other writers might have given their own

CHECK THE POEM
'God's in his heaven, all's right with the world' is the last line of *Pippa's Song*, part of *Pippa Passes* (1841), a long narrative poem by Robert Browning (1812–89). It is the best-known line of the whole work and reflects the Host's attitude to life.

character a more authoritative or important role; Chaucer is happy to make the Host our linking character and guide in the practical matters of the pilgrimage. If Chaucer intends the Host to convey an authorial overview, it might be best summed up as 'have another drink, tell a joke and don't worry'. He is a wonderful creation, his **colloquialism** and rough humour making the Middle Ages seem suddenly so much closer to our own. The Host is many of the things that Chaucer the character is not: active, engaged, prey to changes of temper and emotion.

The pervasiveness of the mood that is created in *The General Prologue* makes it almost impossible to imagine something bad happening to, or being caused by, any of the pilgrims as they travel: the world they move through and inhabit, the world Chaucer creates, is too implicitly full of good human nature to allow this. They may get drunk and abusive, but we feel they will never commit any really heinous crimes so long as they live within the frame of *The Canterbury Tales*. Characters such as the Knight also ensure that the peace is kept between them all. It is the contrast to this pervading sense of good company and humanity that makes the Pardoner's confession seem so dark.

When, in *The General Prologue*, Chaucer joins the others at the Tabard Inn and gives the detailed description of the Pardoner's curious appearance, there is no authorial opinion offered. He merely records the strange costume, hair and lack of beard. When *The Pardoner's Tale* is concluded, he offers no moral judgement on what the Pardoner has confessed. Instead, we get a vivid slice of the Host's vulgarity and temper. It is over in a flash, but it is the perfect end to the darkest and bleakest episode in the whole work. It is a device that allows the work to move on by returning us to the midst of the group of the pilgrims who should, as the Knight points out, 'laughe and pleye' (681). In the final line the pilgrims 'riden forth hir weye' (682) symbolically leaving the dark drama of the Pardoner's Tale behind them.

CHECK THE BOOK
The stage play *The Weir* by Conor Mcpherson (available as a script in *St Nicolas and The Weir*, Nick Hern Books, London, 1997) is based around a **gothic** collection of stories told by four men in a bar which is presided over by a host.

While other contemporary authors, such as William Langland in his poem *Piers Plowman*, created narratives that were focused on explaining a personally-held belief or opinion (or at least the works were designed to convey this sense of authorial honesty) Chaucer's great achievement in *The Canterbury Tales* is the range of voices that come forward to tell their Tale on the dramatic stage that he creates along the road to Canterbury.

LANGUAGE AND STYLE

CHAUCER'S ENGLISH

Chaucer wrote *The Canterbury Tales* in English, a version that we now call Middle English, in order that it could be read by ordinary literate people. If he had, as many other authors did, chosen Latin, the text would have only been accessible to highly educated scholars. He wanted a wide readership and the choice of language matches the content of the Tales: brilliant popular entertainment reflecting (at least in part) real life. In the late fourteenth century court documents were written in Norman French while the Church and scholars wrote in Latin. Neither of these languages was widely understood by the population of England. It was not until 1362 that English became the official language for Parliament and the law courts.

Chaucer lived in a time when most people were illiterate and the spoken word was far more important to them than any written text. Printed books did not exist: all copies of *The Canterbury Tales* dating from Chaucer's time are individual hand-written copies. The rhyme and rhythm of the verse structure of *The Canterbury Tales* makes them highly suited to public telling, which was the usual way in which stories were shared by ordinary people.

Even though it was becoming the most widely used language, English, both spoken and written, varied in different parts of the country. The dialect spoken in the North was different in many points of vocabulary and structure to the dialect of the East Midlands, an area which included London, Oxford and Cambridge. This is the form of English in which Chaucer, as a Londoner, naturally wrote. He understood something of the Northern variations, however, in so far as he has two Northern clerks in *The Reeve's Tale* speaking it.

> **CONTEXT**
>
> Old English, also known as Anglo-Saxon, was spoken (and to a small extent written) between the mid-fifth and the mid-twelfth centuries. Middle English was first spoken after the Norman Invasion (1066) and lasted until the middle of the fifteenth century. After this date a standard form of English slowly developed, based on London dialect English. Its spread was largely due to Caxton using it in all his printed books from 1470 onwards.

THE POETRY OF *THE CANTERBURY TALES*

Like the whole of *The Canterbury Tales*, *The Pardoner's Tale* is written entirely in **rhyming couplets**: each line is an **iambic pentameter**. Of course there are lines which slip from this rigorous form, but the vast majority fit this pattern. Some of the rhymes might not seem quite to work but that is because many words were pronounced differently in Chaucer's day.

The iambic pentameter became the 'standard' line length for much poetry and almost all drama for several centuries after Chaucer. The length suits the breath pattern of someone speaking aloud. Any ten syllable line – regardless of **syntactical** construction, meaning or required dramatic delivery – can be spoken in one breath.

Used without rhyme, poetry written in iambic pentameter became known as **blank verse**. This is the line structure for the vast majority of Shakespeare's plays (and the plays of all other Elizabethan dramatists). However Shakespeare often used just a single rhyming couplet to end a scene: the sound of the rhyme creates an aural sense of rounding off a subject. The last lines of the final scene of *Romeo and Juliet* are a perfect example of this: 'For never was a story of more woe / Than this of Juliet for her Romeo'. (Note that Shakespeare reversed the usual pairing of their names to create the rhyme.)

THE VOICES OF *THE PARDONER'S TALE*

One of the joys of *The Canterbury Tales* is that each Tale is spoken by a different character. This provides enormous variety, even though they all use the same simple poetic structure. Chaucer speaks through the characters; he does not impose an authorial style directly on to the readers. He is as skilled and fluent writing a Tale in the style that the aristocratic Knight would use as he is conveying the sense of gleeful vulgarity in the way the Miller tells his bawdy story. He can swap between pious characters and scoundrels, between men and women, educated and uneducated characters. This gives the various Tales a tremendous sense of vitality and variety.

CHECK THE BOOK

There is a note on the basic rules of pronunciation in the Cambridge edition of *The Pardoner's Tale* on which these Notes are based, just before the actual text.

CHECK THE POEM

Chaucer's lyric poem *Rosamond* uses iambic pentameter but instead of rhyming couplets the rhyme scheme of the eight line verses is ababcdcd.

Most of *The Pardoner's Prologue* and the Tale are spoken by the Pardoner, but there are dramatic sections where he 'quotes' the words of characters in his Tale. These sections create tonal contrast, for example between the angry words of the young men and the humble and polite speech of the old man when they meet.

The Pardoner's natural mode of speaking conveys a sense of a confident, upbeat, fairly well-educated man (he uses a great many biblical and classical references), sure that even his confession of greed and deception will be accepted by the pilgrims. We can imagine he enjoys being the centre of attention. His language is full of vigour and energy. The following sections will help to give you an understanding of how Chaucer achieves this effect.

IMAGERY

For a text that was written over six hundred years ago, the **imagery** that the Pardoner uses sounds fresh, direct and sometimes startlingly graphic. Some of the Pardoner's vivid descriptions of the physical effects of sinning might almost fit into the set of a present day stand-up comedian. This is due partly to the strength and directness of the language Chaucer uses to create his imagery, and partly to the earthy subject matter.

The Miller's Tale contains the best known ribald humour in *The Canterbury Tales*. The English are widely regarded as being perennially fond of crude physical and sexual humour, and many of Chaucer's images featuring this bawdiness would not be out of place in contemporary knockabout risqué comedy. Traditional pantomime also employs performance devices that borrow from the spirit if not the actual stories of many of Chaucer's Tales: people in disguise, deceptions, comic physical misadventures, for example. Most of the vivid physical imagery in *The Pardoner's Tale* is not, however, used for slapstick comic effect but to create disgusting images of excess and decay to make sinners ashamed. It is used to enhance his **rhetorical** tone, and to develop the macabre, **gothic** mood of the writing.

 CHECK THE BOOK
Chaucer did not always match his style to the character as well as he does in *The Pardoner's Tale*. The short *Shipman's Tale* does not seem to reveal the voice of an uncouth mariner. It is generally held that Chaucer wrote this snippet of narrative for *The Wife of Bath* then reassigned it but didn't revise it to suit the new speaker.

CONTEXT

Comedy was inherent in most types of medieval drama, rather than a specific **genre** as it tends to be today. The **Saints plays** of the early Middle Ages (for example, *Mary Magdalen*, c. 1500) and the Morality plays of the later all involved large elements of comedy despite their apparently serious themes and content.

The most intense passage of vivid, earthy images occurs when the Pardoner sets out, very successfully, to convey the grossness and corruption of gluttony. In a furious passage (238–60) he describes the actions of eating and of preparing food in a way that makes this natural function seem revolting. The drinker makes his throat a privy or toilet. His 'bely' is a pod full of dung and corruption, and foul sounds emanate from either end of the glutton's body. When the Pardoner moves on to describe cooks preparing food, the scene he paints is of coarse physical labour described with verbs like 'stamp', 'strain', 'grind' and 'knock'. Nothing is thrown away in this process of rendering down ingredients to make the glutton's sauce. It is a very powerful passage, inviting revulsion at the thought of food.

The Pardoner uses similarly energetic and condemnatory language to create vivid depictions of the behaviour of sinners. In the conclusion to his tirade against 'hasardrye' or gambling (304–73) he imagines frantic gamblers blaspheming as they prepare to throw dice – " 'By Goddes precious herte', and 'by his nailes,"' (365). Then, in their fury, they warn the imaginary opponent that if they attempt to cheat 'this daggere shal thurghout thyn herte go' (369). The voice the Pardoner creates for these gamblers is frantic and aggressive. The Pardoner 'caps' this blaspheming voice by invoking 'the love of Crist' (372) himself, but juxtaposing the evils of gambling with Christ's love as a positive thing.

CONTEXT

Gambling was a sin that for many Christians would remind them of one of the darkest details of the crucifixion, the guards throwing dice for Jesus's clothes while he was dying on the cross.

Chaucer uses a number of simple but effective visual images in the Tale itself. The most symbolic of these is the 'croked wey' (475) along which the old man says the young men will find death. They follow not only the literal crooked path to the treasure but also a morally crooked way of dealing with one another, which leads to their deaths. The old man is described as 'al forwrapped' (432) almost as if disguised. The bottles that the young man who goes to town fills with poisoned wine are described as 'large' (585) and 'grete' (591). He knows that his friends have great thirsts for alcohol, but he wants to ensure they die, and he is like a man who chooses the biggest weapon in an armoury to demonstrate his desire to kill.

ALLUSION

One of the things that strikes, and equally may confuse, many modern readers is the number of references or **allusions** the Pardoner makes to the Bible and to classical authors and their stories. Today a poet might seek to express an idea through striking, original **imagery** and would usually opt not to make references to other stories and sources that might slow down the uninformed reader. But in Chaucer's day the use of allusions was regarded as something that readers enjoyed. It was a display of intelligence undertaken not, we imagine, for the vanity of the author, but for the engagement of the reader. The author assumed that educated readers – a very small and intellectually cohesive proportion of the population – would have all read some of the same books. The Bible would be the prime assumed source of shared knowledge, with key stories from the Old and New Testaments studied by readers, all of whom would have been educated on Christian principles.

The Pardoner uses many allusions to support his own opinions, chiefly about the effects of sinning. We can imagine that he is incorporating allusions and references to show the pilgrims how educated and knowledgeable he is. One or two of his references are obscure, perhaps to ensure that none of the other pilgrims will know all his sources. For example, he refers to 'Stilboun' (317), who is a character from a story related by John of Salisbury in a book written in Latin about two centuries before Chaucer's pilgrims are imagined to be making their journey.

Allusion is not employed consistently throughout the text. Using allusion in the foreground of a story – rather than allowing it to be implied through things that are part of the direct narrative flow – generally slows down the dramatic pace of a narrative, and opens up the focus of the writing away from the subject and on to the themes. Chaucer knows exactly where and when to use allusions for both linguistic and dramatic effect. They would, for example, slow down the onward rush of the closing stages of the Tale towards its violent conclusion, and are therefore omitted from this section of the Tale.

> **CONTEXT**
>
> In *The Story of English* (Cran, MacNeil and McCrum, Penguin revised edition, 2003), the authors suggest that many people went to church to hear lengthy **sermons** as much for entertainment as for spiritual instruction.

Equally, there are no obvious **allusions** to the Bible or to classical authors in the whole Prologue, though when the Pardoner refers to not making 'baskettes' for his livelihood (159) he is alluding to St Paul the Hermit who made baskets for a living. It could be that the Pardoner, who is probably not as educated as the allusions he has learnt specifically for his sermon suggest, is confusing this little known St Paul with the much better known apostle St Paul. Apart from this, the Prologue is very focused and economically written. The Pardoner covers a lot of ground in it and does not need to employ allusions to support what is a very personal statement – a confession – of what he does and why. It could be argued that he has less need to impress listeners with a display of knowledge in the Prologue than he does in the rest of the Tale, especially in those sections where he demonstrates his **sermonising** skills (see **Part Three: Structure**).

QUESTION
Do you think the language of the Pardoner's sermon against sins is designed purely to shock and provoke disgust, or is he using devices intended to amuse as well?

In the 'demonstration' sermon against sin in the Tale itself (197–374) allusions are a key part of the tone and style of the language. 'Looth' (Lot) and Herod from the Bible and Seneca the Latin writer from the first century AD are all quickly mentioned in the opening lines of the sermon (199–211). (Like the other significant allusions throughout the Tale, these are explained in more detail in the relevant sections of the summaries in **Part Two** of these Notes.) References to other texts were an important part of a sermon, so the Pardoner is doing what the pilgrims would expect. Yet, given what we know of his proud nature, he may also be showing off his wide knowledge for its own sake.

There are further groupings of allusions throughout the sermon (in addition to those mentioned above):

- Attila and Samuel/Lamuel at the end of the Pardoner's second attack on drunkenness (293–302).

- Matthew and 'Jeremye' (Jeremiah) from the Bible again (349–351).

When the Pardoner returns to his actual Tale, the only 'allusions' to recognisable biblical figures are within curses invoking 'seinte Marie' (399) (St Mary) and 'Seint John' (466) until the very end of the Tale when he mentions 'Avycen' (603). This is an allusion to Avicenna, the Latinised form of the name Ibn Sina, an Arab scientist and philosopher who was relatively well-known to educated Europeans because of his great medical knowledge.

After the Tale itself, the Pardoner condemns sin directly (609–13) with a fury indicated by a flurry of exclamation marks. Involving any allusions here would reduce dramatic impact. The final allusion is at line 665, where the furious Host invokes 'Seint Eleyne' and the 'crois' she found. This is a reference to St Helena, who was supposed to have discovered the actual cross on which Christ was crucified. It may seem odd that the rough and ready Host can so readily quote a rather obscure saint. It may be that Chaucer is writing slightly out of the Host's character here, or it may be that knowledge of St Helena was more commonplace in an age that venerated relics.

RHETORIC

Unlike most of the other pilgrims, the Pardoner is a practised and professional public speaker. We see he is eager to be called upon to tell a Tale, and can imagine the pilgrims gathering round someone who they hope will have the skill to produce something above average for their entertainment. They may get more than they bargain for in terms of what the Pardoner happily reveals about himself, by his apparent total lack of guilt, conscience or shame. They certainly get a confession, sermon and Tale delivered in powerful, energetic and vivid language: the hallmarks of the Pardoner's tone of speech.

As befits a passionate sermon, many images and phrases the Pardoner employs are extravagant, urgent and intense. Look at the number of exclamation marks in the sermon section of the Tale especially. Gluttony is full of 'cursednesse', causes 'confusioun' and 'dampnacioun' (damnation) and each of these gets its own exclamation mark (212–4). This is clearly passionate rhetorical language powerfully delivered.

> **CONTEXT**
>
> **Rhetoric** was considered a necessary skill for a scholar to study in the Middle Ages. It formed, with grammar and logic, the Trivium, the lower division of the Seven Liberal Arts. (The Quadrivium, or higher division, consisted of arithmetic, geometry, astronomy and music.)

RHETORIC continued

**CHECK
THE BOOK**
John webster's
**gothic revenge
tragedy** *The White
Devil* (1612), is full
of rhetorical
language, as all the
characters deceive
and manipulate
each other for their
own ends. It has an
extremely complex
plot and much of
what the central
characters say
cannot be taken
at face value.

The Pardoner's energetic tone is not restricted to the demonstration sermon section of the Tale. When he explains in the Prologue what he does, how he cheats poor churchgoers out their money, his tone is forceful, even, we might think, to his own disadvantage. He certainly does not apologise or play down what he does. He is confident and strident enough to say that he is always ready to take money from the 'povereste' (poorest) page or widow in a village (163–4). This is part of a powerful expression of his greed: we can imagine the shock this produces among the pilgrims.

One of the 'tricks' of good **rhetorical** performance is to speak directly to the audience. The Pardoner does this at several points. He 'shows' (we can imagine he might actually get the object from his bag and holds it up) the fake miraculous mitten to the pilgrims (86). He encourages them to listen closely at the end of his Prologue (168) to the Tale he is about to tell. He introduces each of the sins with a remark to the pilgrims explaining his move into a new subject, for example lines 300–3 (rounding off his attack on gluttony), and line 341 when he says he will now turn to speaking against oaths and blasphemy. He employs the rhetorical device of addressing the audience directly to re-engage any who might not be listening closely. He tells them he has a Tale still to tell at line 374, and asks them a rhetorical question (that is, a question asked for effect, not really wanting an answer) at the deliberately brief and focused swift conclusion of the Tale itself – 'What nedeth it to sermone of it moore?' (593). All these devices engage the pilgrims and give *The Pardoner's Tale* its drive and energy.

PART FOUR

CRITICAL PERSPECTIVES

READING CRITICALLY

This section provides a range of critical viewpoints and perspectives on *The Pardoner's Tale* and gives a broad overview of key debates, interpretations and theories proposed since the Tale was published. It is important to bear in mind the variety of interpretations and responses this text has produced, many of them shaped by the critics' own backgrounds and historical contexts.

No single view of the text should be seen as dominant – it is important that you arrive at your own judgements by questioning the perspectives described, and by developing your own critical insights. Objective analysis is a skill achieved through coupling close reading with an informed understanding of the key ideas, related texts and background information relevant to the text. These elements are all crucial in enabling you to assess the interpretations of other readers, and even to view works of criticism as texts in themselves. The ability to read critically will serve you well both in your study of the text, and in any critical writing, presentation, or further work you undertake.

ORIGINAL RECEPTION

The Canterbury Tales is a very early work of English Literature and it is difficult for us to assess its effect on readers when it first appeared. There were no critics publishing reviews in newspapers or magazines. Indeed, there were no printed books so we cannot say how popular *The Canterbury Tales* was, based on publishing figures. However, over eighty near-contemporary hand-made copies of *The Canterbury Tales* made during Chaucer's lifetime have survived, a remarkably high number, which suggests that the work was a medieval 'best seller' as soon as it appeared.

> **CONTEXT**
>
> As well as book and film versions of *The Canterbury Tales*, Chaucer has inspired musicians. In 1961 composer Erik Chisholm wrote an opera based on three of the Tales. The second act is a musical version of *The Pardoner's Tale*.

The Canterbury Tales was one of the first texts that William Caxton printed on his presses in 1478, eighty years after Chaucer's death, indicating that the work was still very popular. The Tales have been in print ever since. Their influence upon other writers and artists has been enormous.

LATER CRITICISM

CONTEXT

John Dryden (1631–1700) was a poet and playwright who enjoyed great success and published a large number of books. He was appointed Poet Laureate in 1668 and wrote fourteen plays between that date and 1681. His best known play is *All for Love*, a version of the story of Antony and Cleopatra written in **blank verse**.

Pre-twentieth century critics of *The Canterbury Tales* often appear to confuse morality with aesthetics: what they criticise or ignore in Chaucer are those elements that offend their moral principles and sensibilities. The poet and playwright John Dryden did much to promote the works of Chaucer, but he always avoided any of the bawdy material because he felt it was his intellectual and artistic duty to instruct rather than merely please. (Chaucer probably felt exactly the reverse.) Dryden produced his own version of *Troilus and Cressida* (with his own spelling of their names) in 1679.

Joseph Strutt was an artist and scholar who wrote *Dresses and Habits of the English People* (1799) in which he condemned the behaviour of the pilgrims in *The Canterbury Tales*. He treated them as if they were real people who were abusing the religious notion of a pilgrimage. These characters were, in his moral opinion, 'deficient in morality and some few (of them) outrageous to common decency'. Even in the twentieth century the poet Robert Graves (whose personality mixed English upper middle class and bohemian creative elements in equal measure) commented that many of the bawdy stories told by the less morally upright pilgrims in *The Canterbury Tales* revealed that Chaucer himself had 'criminal sympathies'.

 CHECK THE BOOK

The poet Robert Graves's (1895–1985) autobiography *Goodbye to All That* (1929) is a powerful statement of disillusion with the politics and philosophy that caused so many to die in the First World War.

It seems that for many centuries Chaucer has been criticised for creating realistic characters whose stories do not always contain a clear worthy moral message. He has effectively been criticised for what we now regard as his greatest achievement: the realistic portrayal of a wide cast of characters, from nobles to fraudsters. Perhaps what these critics really objected to was the fact that Chaucer does not condemn the morally reprehensible characters he creates, nor do they, on the pilgrimage at least, suffer any bad consequences as a result of their laxities and villainy. In fact, apart from the Pardoner, they are not particularly villainous: in current police terms the worst of them would be classified as 'petty criminals'.

CONTEMPORARY APPROACHES

Critical reading means stepping back from the text as an entertainment and looking at ways to explore and examine its deeper ideas and effects. Various schools of critical study have developed to encompass key types of approach to studying literature – such as Marxist, Humanist and Dramatic critical approaches and Feminist or gender studies. Three out of four of these approaches are discussed below. *The Pardoner's Tale* is less studied by feminist critics because it has no significant female characters. The only remark the Pardoner makes about women is, perhaps not surprisingly, unfavourable. At line 191 he describes the arrival at the inn of 'tombersteres', dancing girls 'whiche been the verray develes officeres', the very devil's officers (194). It is his only reference to the sin of lust, apart from the implication that wine is the cause of lechery (263).

MARXIST CRITICISM

Marxist criticism focuses on interpreting evidence from the text that suggests plot, character and actions are motivated by tension between social classes and between populations and economic power bases. A Marxist critical approach to *The Miller's Tale* would, for example, see beyond the bawdy comedy and personal motives to a struggle between characters representing the professional classes with those from the working class. They would see the fact that Nicholas from the professional class gets his backside branded in a comic trick as the revenge of the working masses upon a subjugating 'superior' class.

Marxist criticism explores the economic needs that drive characters in many of *The Canterbury Tales*, and sees class struggle as a motivation for the actions of many characters. They would read the Pardoner as a man who uses the means at his disposal, however corruptly, to survive in a system that keeps people economically subjugated. They would perhaps regard him less critically than other commentators

CHECK THE BOOK

Two excellent books on Feminist criticism of Chaucer are *Chaucer's Approach to Gender in The Canterbury Tales*, Anna Laskaya (Cambridge, 1995), an in-depth study of Chaucer's attitudes to gender and male/female roles; and *Feminising Chaucer*, Jill Mann (Boydell and Brewer, 2002) which reviews Chaucer's handling of gender issues and **misogynistic** stereotypes.

CHECK THE NET
The German political philosopher and revolutionary Karl Marx (1818–83) wrote 'religion is the opiate of the masses' though it is usually misquoted as '*opium* of the masses'. It is not from his major work *Das Kapital* (1867), but from the introduction to his *Critique of Hegel's Philosophy of Right*. For an overview of Marx's work and theories, go to **www.historyguide. org/intellect/marx. html**

CHECK THE BOOK
The best known contemporary Marxist literary critic is Terry Eagleton. In 1986 he published *Geoffrey Chaucer* (Blackwell) with co-author Stephen Knight. They looked at Marxist interpretations of several of *The Canterbury Tales*, particularly the Miller's, Clerk's and Reeve's tales.

who focus more on the Pardoner's flawed personal morality than imagining (we have to imagine because we do not know any details of his life beyond the things he tells us) the circumstances that have forced the Pardoner to do what he does to survive.

Marxist political philosophy casts organised religion as essentially a repressive institution. Marxist literary criticism sees the medieval Church primarily as a social-human power structure. It held enormous power over people both spiritually and, crucially, economically. Despite the apparent need for money to be gained from the sale of pardons, the Church was still a fabulously wealthy organisation in the Middle Ages. Many senior churchmen lived in palaces and enjoyed a lifestyle similar to the nobility, and the Church owned and ran vast rural estates. The Pardoner can be seen, from a Marxist perspective, as someone who infiltrates this powerful socio-economic organisation, ignores its spiritual dimension and uses his skill to extract personal gain from it. Unfortunately, he is far from being a perfect model of a 'moral robber' (like, for example, the imagined version of Robin Hood who stole from the rich to give to the poor) because he doesn't relieve the Church itself of any wealth, but diverts the income stream it relied on from poor believers to his own pocket.

HUMANIST CRITICISM

Humanist criticism identifies aspects of medieval literature which illuminate the essential human condition over and above particular historical influences. The enduring appeal of *The Canterbury Tales*, and the fact that six centuries after they were written they still provide excellent and credible dramatic frameworks for modern versions, suggests that Chaucer's ability to unfold creatively the human condition is his greatest achievement.

A key aspect you might study to develop a humanist reading of *The Pardoner's Tale* is Chaucer's dramatic use of voices, of direct speech, throughout the text. Despite the potential limit of a simple and rigorous line length and **rhyming couplet** structure, *The Pardoner's Tale* is alive with striking and diverse voices: the gleeful Pardoner who skilfully balances 'confession' and pride, the aggressive young revellers and their curses and the dark, mysterious speech of the Old Man.

DRAMATIC CRITICISM

Some critics have chosen to read *The Canterbury Tales* as primarily a work of drama rather than a narrative poem. Chaucer's skill in the creation and presentation of characters is central to this approach. Although in critically interpreting some of the Tales this approach can ignore the importance of narrative structure, dramatic criticism does provide an interesting way to consider Chaucer's creation of his cast of characters. The links between Tales, the interconnections between characters from one Tale or narrative episode to the next, are important to this critical approach.

Dramatic criticism would also consider what now might be regarded as the theatrical elements that run through most of the Tales. There is a sense of carnival and of knockabout physical comedy in many of the stories – which is why they have lent themselves so well to dramatisation on stage or screen. The theatrical notion of costume and dressing up also features in the Tales, as do ambiguous gender roles.

Dramatic criticism is particularly appropriate to the character of the Pardoner. He is a performer. His 'demonstration **sermon**' resembles an actor conducting a master class, revealing how he creates his role. The whole Prologue and Tale is built around his demonstrating his skill as a public speaker to the pilgrims. His 'costume' and physical appearance is so striking that it is commented on in great detail in *The General Prologue*. His gender is regarded as being ambiguous. These aspects of his physicality could be regarded as theatrical, part of his role as a performer to congregations.

> **CONTEXT**
>
> In 1995, the Royal Shakespeare Company put on a production of *The Canterbury Tales*, including The *Pardoner's Tale*, using a mixture of modern and Middle English, and colourful props and costumes.

PART FIVE

BACKGROUND

GEOFFREY CHAUCER'S LIFE AND WORKS

Geoffrey Chaucer was born – as far as we know – in 1343 in London. The name Chaucer is thought to derive from the French '*chaussier*' suggesting that at some time the family made shoes, but Chaucer's father John was a prosperous wine merchant operating in London. This may explain the detailed references to the wine trade that Chaucer brings into the Pardoner's 'demonstration **sermon**' (277–86).

We do not have many details of Chaucer's early life but we know that by 1357, when he was still in his teens, he was in service in some capacity in the household of the Countess of Ulster. Two years later he went off to France as a soldier in the war against the French, which started when England's king Edward III made an (unsuccessful) bid to claim the French throne. At this time, England did not maintain a professional army of full-time soldiers. When a war required fighting men, people joined up. Gentlemen and nobles usually did so in the hope of gaining preferment and grants of money or positions of power from the grateful king when the fighting was over. Peasants joined because they were encouraged to or were coerced by the lord of the land where they lived and worked, or because their lives were so hard they thought they might fare better in the army. For many people ordinary life was lived at subsistence level and a spell in the army might offer them more chance of excitement and wealth (through plunder of the enemy or reward from grateful commanders) than life working the land.

Chaucer was captured by the French at Reims. He was considered by the enemy to be enough of a gentleman to be worth ransoming (see **Part One: Reading** *The Pardoner's Tale*) and the next year, 1360, the king contributed £16 to Chaucer's ransom fee.

In 1365 Chaucer married Philippa Pan de Roet, a woman of high social standing. The following year he was sent to Spain on a diplomatic mission. This was the start of a long period of various

> **CONTEXT**
>
> Chaucer's employer, the Countess of Ulster (an Irish title but her household was in England) was married to Prince Lionel, son of Edward III, who in 1569 raised a troop of men, including Chaucer, to fight, unsuccessfully as it turned out, against the French.

public offices held by Chaucer. It is likely that he was appointed to several official positions because of the knowledge and learning he so clearly displayed. Some of the official journeys he was sent on were considered secret diplomatic missions.

For most of his life Chaucer was enough of a public figure for his fortunes to be linked to the court of the reigning king, but he was not so much one king's man that he would automatically be ruined if they were deposed. This autonomy was important because the throne of England was in dispute throughout most of Chaucer's life.

Chaucer fared well under Edward III, who had ruled since 1321, over twenty years before Chaucer was born. Edward granted Chaucer a life pension for services rendered in 1367. Chaucer went on an eleven month diplomatic mission to Italy in 1372–3. He then appears to have combined public positions at home in England (he was appointed Controller of the Customs and Subsidy of Wools, Skins and Leather, for example, a post in which he oversaw the taxation of goods in 1374) with further secret political missions abroad to Flanders, Lombardy and Italy. In 1377 when Edward died and was succeeded by Richard II, his grandson, Chaucer was sent to France to negotiate for peace with the French king Charles V.

As he grew older, Chaucer was employed in public service more frequently in England: on several secret missions in the late 1370s, then more openly as a Justice of the Peace in Kent in 1385. There was an interruption to his career when Richard II was deprived of power in 1386 and Chaucer lost all his official posts. His wife Philippa died the following year. By 1388 Chaucer, for reasons that are not entirely clear, was so poor he had to sell his life pensions to raise money. Fortunately Richard regained power in 1389 and shortly afterwards Chaucer was made Clerk of the King's Works and Deputy Forester of the royal forest of North Petherton in Somerset. As well as payment for all these public administrative posts, Chaucer was granted money and life pensions from various noble figures. It should have been the economic foundations of a comfortable old age.

Records show that in 1380 a charge of rape made by one Cecily Chaumpaigne against Chaucer was withdrawn just before the court

CHECK THE BOOK

The Life of Geoffrey Chaucer by Derek Pearsell (Blackwell, 1982) is a detailed biography of Chaucer's life.

hearing was due. Such evidence as we have of this affair suggest that Chaumpaigne withdrew her accusation because she heard of the many great and powerful gentlemen Chaucer had arranged to speak in court in defence of his character and reputation. It is not clear who Chaumpaigne was, nor if Chaucer's wife Philippa knew of the alleged incident before the accusation was made. At this time Philippa was known to be absent from home for long periods and was almost certainly having an affair with John of Gaunt, one of the most powerful men in England and known to Chaucer. Chaucer talks of his son Louis (or Lewis) being born in 1381, almost exactly nine months after the rape was alleged to have taken place, but there is no further evidence to suggest the boy's mother might have been Cecily Chaumpaigne.

Whether Chaucer did rape Cecily Chaumpaigne and then used his powerful social connections to avoid a court case has been the subject of much speculation, especially in regard to the attitudes revealed in his writing. Many of Chaucer's works feature degrees of **misogyny**. The possibility that he was a rapist makes critics wonder to what extent he was merely reflecting the common misogynistic attitudes of his times in his fiction, or whether he himself was displaying a particularly high degree of personally held disdain for women.

Chaucer did not travel abroad during the last decade of his life. He lived in Greenwich in London and money seems to have continued to be a problem for him. He wrote several 'begging poems' but it is by no means clear exactly what his financial situation was. Richard II, who appears to have favoured him, was again forced from the throne in 1399, and died in prison the following year. Chaucer, however, took a new house in 1399, in the garden of Westminster Abbey, a very prestigious and expensive address, suggesting he was again financially secure. Chaucer died the following year in 1400. He was buried in Westminster Abbey, where a monument to him was erected in 1555.

CHAUCER'S OTHER WORKS

Despite the range of Chaucer's writing, we can identify six main story types recurring throughout his work. This is not to identify a limitation, but shows how many main types of story he was

CHECK THE BOOK

Novelist and literary biographer Peter Ackroyd (b. 1949) has written a series of very accessible literary biographies that form his 'Brief Lives' series. His *Chaucer (Brief Lives)* (Vintage, 2005) contains an account of the alleged rape incident.

confident he could tell, nearly always successfully. These six story types are as follows:

Courtly romance – tales that revolve around love and 'noble' issues like war and honour in a stylised, courtly setting. *The Canterbury Tales, The Knight's Tale* and *The Wife of Bath's Tale* are examples of this sort of work. Chaucer's other best-known work, *Troilus and Criseyde*, is a **courtly romance**.

Lives of holy figures – in tone and sometimes content these are similar to courtly romances. They are dramatically stylised and focused on to virtuous behaviour, but the heroes are holy figures rather than knights, ladies or nobles. The conclusion of such stories often involves a heroine defeating evil, even though she is usually martyred in the process. Several of *The Canterbury Tales* feature such lives. Virginia is 'martyred' by her father to preserve her honour in *The Physician's Tale*. *The Second Nun's Prologue and Tale* tells the story of the martyrdom and subsequent canonisation of the virginal and devout Cecilia. The Parson in his Tale talks at great length – his story is more of a solemn and formal **sermon** – of the kind of pious life that must be led in order to gain admittance to heaven.

Fabliau – comic tales built around an extended trick usually enacted by a cast of characters from the lower ends of society. The bawdy and knockabout *Miller's Tale* is a great and lively example of this story type.

Sermon – delivered in church, these were complex and often highly **rhetorical** lectures encouraging congregations to embrace holy behaviour and to listen to the commands of the Church. Chaucer knew that for many people sermons were the closest they came to hearing poetry and stories told with style and flourish. Chaucer has characters deliver sermons in three of *The Canterbury Tales: The Pardoner's Tale, The Nun's Priest's Prologue* and *The Parson's Tale*.

Confession – the most formal use of a confession story-form in the sense of characters revealing (though not apologising for) their sins in all of Chaucer's work is *The Pardoner's Tale*. Elements of confession appear in many of his other works, including *The Wife of Bath's Tale*.

 CHECK THE NET
Go to the British Library website to find details – including facsimile pages – of a lavishly ornamented fourteenth century hand-written manuscript copy of *The Canterbury Tales*. Go to **www.bl.uk** and search for 'Canterbury Tales'.

The moral tale – a common type of writing used by Chaucer, a little like a sermon but designed to be read rather than listened to. Often **allegorical** in form, **moral tales** from the medieval period can seem rather tedious and stiff to us. They are concerned with the virtues and vices, with heaven and hell; with people being tested by life's problems and injustices and knowing how to make the morally right choice. Such tales appear throughout Chaucer's works. They form the core of two of Chaucer's other major works: *Boece*, Chaucer's translation of Boethius's long poem *The Consolations of Philosophy* (the autobiography of a sixth century Roman noble), and *The Romance of the Rose*, a highly creative 'translation' based on the work of two French authors who never actually met (see below). The Tale the Pardoner tells is highly moral, but it is built around a folk tale that is much more lively and dramatically driven than most straightforward moral tales. They tended to be more like lectures than stories.

Despite his busy life, Chaucer was always working at his writing, but we do not know the exact sequence in which he wrote his main works. Critics commonly divide his writing into three phases defined by the dominant poetic form he used in each (though they differ slightly over the exact dates of each phase):

The early period – 1359–72, also known as the period of French influence (because Chaucer was studying French literature and writing translations of some French texts as well as his own poetry). In this phase of his career, Chaucer was mainly using the octosyllabic couplet – rhymed pairs of lines with eight syllables in each line. Key works from this period include:

The Book of the Duchess – written for John of Gaunt, son of Edward III, on the death of his first wife Duchess Blanche of Castile (later of Lancaster) in 1369. This long formal poem features a lengthy description of the poet as narrator, that is, of Chaucer himself. The poem is inspired by a desire to memorialise Duchess Blanche and console her bereaved husband, who was probably an acquaintance of Chaucer's.

The Romance of the Rose (1370?) – a **courtly romance** with strong moral themes and an allegorical style, this is Chaucer's

---

CONTEXT

Chaucer appears as the poet or the narrator in many of his works, beginning with *The Book of the Duchess* where the first four hundred lines are devoted entirely to creating his character. Chaucer as poet/narrator also appears in *The Parliament of Fowls, The House of Fame, Troilus and Criseyde* and the *General Prologue* of *The Canterbury Tales*.

translation of a long French poem *Le Roman de la Rose* begun by a young French courtier, Guillaume de Lorris, around 1237. He never completed it, and it was picked up later by Jean de Meun, who turned the original highly stylised and symbolic poem into a **satire** on stiff formal court manners. There are gently satirical aspects in Chaucer's treatment of the story.

The ABC of the Virgin – also known as *Chaucer's ABC*, this poem is an **acrostic**, in that it has twenty-three arranged alphabetically according to the medieval Latin alphabet by the first letter of each verse. It merges praise for a beautiful and devout woman with praise for the Virgin Mary. It may have been written at the request of Duchess Blanche (see *The Book of the Duchess* above).

The middle period – 1372–86, which is also known as the period of Italian influence because Chaucer was studying the Italian writers Dante and Boccaccio. Chaucer moves in this prolific period from the octosyllabic couplet to the **heroic couplet** (a pair of rhymed **iambic pentameters**) that dominates his later work. Key works from this period include:

Troilus and Criseyde – also alternatively spelt *Troylus and Cryseyde* and sometimes attributed to 1385, just before his third period, this is Chaucer's other great and best known work. A long and complex courtly romance set in classical times but featuring what are clearly medieval characters and concepts. The main characters are knights and ladies and the poem presents a chivalric vision of love and war.

The Parliament of Fowls, *The House of Fame* and *The Legend of the Good Woman* – these are all basically court romances, featuring highly idealised love stories set in noble courts. Life in these poems is seen as an elaborate series of rituals. Each of these works extends beyond the form of the court romance, however, as Chaucer adds various elements such as moral tracts (a discourse on 'the common good' before the main narrative in *The Parliament of Fowls* for example) as well as interludes of low-life comedy that contrast with the formal courtly passages. The main narrative in each of these poems is only introduced after all sorts of preparatory material: incidental stories, personal

 CHECK THE BOOK Shakespeare wrote his own version of the story of the lovers *Troilus and Criseyde* in his play *Troilus and Cressida*, written almost exactly two hundred years after Chaucer's death.

comments and philosophical musings. It is in the introductory sections of each of these works that Chaucer widens the range about which he is writing – just as he does on a smaller scale in the lengthy Prologue and the demonstration **sermon** before the actual story in *The Pardoner's Tale*.

In this period, Chaucer also produced early drafts of some stories that would later appear in *The Canterbury Tales*.

The third period – 1386–1400, also known as his mature period, in which he more or less exclusively writes in the **heroic couplet** form. Key works from this period include:

The Canterbury Tales – begun 1386 and uncompleted at his death.

Boece – a translation of Boethius's *The Consolations of Philosophy*. This was the fictionalised and dramatised autobiography of a sixth century Roman noble. He is imprisoned and there visited by a vision called 'Lady Philosophy' who consoles him even as he is executed.

A Treatise on the Astrolabe – this is a practical step-by-step instruction on how to use the astrolabe, a hand-held mechanical device that demonstrated the movement and positions of the stars. This was highly sophisticated technology in Chaucer's time. The work is dedicated to a little boy called Louis, probably Chaucer's son.

> **CONTEXT**
>
> It is not known whether Chaucer actually possessed his own astrolabe. Several museums and institutions have claimed to have the very astrolabe he owned but the British Museum convincingly suggests that most of the astrolabes that have survived (including theirs) were probably built by people who had read Chaucer's excellent text.

LITERARY BACKGROUND

THE GOTHIC TRADITION IN LITERATURE

Any work of literature deemed to be **gothic** in content or style commonly includes at least some of the following elements:

- The supernatural, usually in malign form.

- Elements that work specifically to create a sense of terror and fear, felt either by characters within the gothic story or by the readers, or both.

- The breaking of conventional moral or ethical codes, usually with some hint of spiritual, moral or sexual perversity (as in things that are 'against the natural order').

- A (possibly unhealthy) focus on the macabre in the detailed setting of the story.

Key texts that might give an understanding of these gothic conventions include Marlowe's stage play *Dr Faustus* (1604), which contains the supernatural figure of Mephistopheles, an agent from the devil who comes to tempt (successfully) Faustus to give his soul to the devil in exchange for earthly powers.

Shakespeare's shortest play and most popular tragedy, *Macbeth* (1603), is another masterpiece of stage drama with a strong gothic element. The violent action of the play is started by the mysterious and fatally misinterpreted predictions of three witches. Both their messages to Macbeth, and the promises of the supernatural Mephistopheles in *Dr Faustus*, are examples of wishes granted to characters who do not understand the true, darker consequences inherent in the wish. These devices precisely echo the way the three men search for death and find it, but not in the way they expected, in *The Pardoner's Tale*.

Many regard Horace Walpole's novel *The Castle of Otranto: A Gothic Story* (1769) as the first great gothic novel: it contains every element of the genre in abundance. Mary Shelley's novel *Frankenstein* (1818) and Bram Stoker's *Dracula* (1897) both work to create a sense of fear and horror in their readers by creating, in *Dracula*, a supernatural figure, and in *Frankenstein* an unnatural figure in the monster which has been created by human hands rather than nature. Webster's violent and claustrophobic gothic plays *The Duchess of Malfi* (1614) and *The White Devil* (1612), and Emily Brontë's intense and darkly passionate novel *Wuthering Heights* (1847) all feature characters who are driven by sexual passion to form relationships that break social or moral codes. In all three cases death is one result of the events and circumstances. All these gothic texts focus on the macabre to a greater or lesser degree in terms of their settings: none locates its action in a bright world of sunshine, innocence and human delight. *The Canterbury Tales* were

CHECK THE BOOK
Gothic elements can be present in works that fall within other **genres** of prose fiction. Many critics regard Daphne du Maurier's epic period romance *Jamaica Inn* (1936) to be strongly gothic in tone. Arriving for the first time at the eponymous remote Cornish Inn, the heroine of the story sees the ramshackle sign hanging like a gibbet. Details like this are strongly gothic in mood.

CHECK THE NET
The BBC website has an excellent variety of pages on the Middle Ages, including articles on the Black Death and the gothic architecture of Britain's cathedrals and churches. Go to **www.bbc.co.uk** and search for 'medieval'.

written two hundred years before the earliest of these **gothic** works (Marlowe's *Dr Faustus*) yet we can see elements of the gothic in *The Pardoner's Tale*.

The term 'gothic' means, among other things, inspired by arts or images from the Middle Ages. Chaucer does not perceive his world as gothic in the way that the later writers do. They see it as something that has a style and atmosphere different from the world in which they actually live. For Chaucer, those elements in his work were just part of his everyday world or the culture that surrounded his own creative work. Furthermore, the good humour and fellowship that often shines out from *The Canterbury Tales*, as personified in *The Pardoner's Tale* by the Host, are definitely not gothic elements.

In *The Pardoner's Tale* what exactly can we identify as gothic elements? Working through the list at the start of this section we can see that:

- The supernatural is present in the form of the mysterious old man. Is he Death personified, Death's supernatural agent or some strange once-human creature who is now cursed not to die?

- Although none of the characters in the Tale appears to feel fear, the Pardoner attempts to create an air of menace over the three young men and hopes that some of what they do not feel will be experienced by some of the pilgrims.

- The Pardoner breaks, through his life of deception, the religious codes of the day. He is mocking and abusing the Christian faith of those he cheats. He may also be, in some unspecified way, breaking sexual norms. Does his strange appearance indicate a castrated man or a woman in man's guise? Or even an hermaphrodite? Furthermore, it might be argued that *The Pardoner's Tale* implies that the three young sinners also break socio-religious conventions through their habitual wickedness and are punished – in gothic style – by sudden and violent death.

- The setting for the **moral tale**, a plague-ravaged countryside, is overshadowed by a macabre air, stalked by the figure of Death and by funerals. More macabre to us, but perhaps not to

Chaucer's readers, is the continual references to the relics that the Pardoner handles. Reverence for bones, rags and scraps of body parts seems grisly, even perverse to us, and certainly fulfils the later gothic fashion for things unhealthy, sepulchral and frankly revolting. However, though we might squeamishly shrink from the idea of worshipping a human bone, Chaucer's pilgrims did not, and the idea of including such funereal items in gothic literature specifically to make the reader's flesh creep, is a creation of later gothic writers.

VERSE NARRATIVES

Chaucer was writing several centuries before the novel was invented as a literary form, the book-length narrative story written in prose. He used heroic couplets to tell stories. Today, most poetry or 'verse' is written as some form of personal lyric. The poet expresses a personally held opinion, or relates, explores and intellectually develops a personally experienced event. Most poems are quite short, few exceeding half a dozen pages, most being considerably shorter. Poetry is now a very distinct different literary form from prose fiction. Very few modern poets write narrative verse, though some write sequences of linked poems that together tell a story.

Today most writers who want to tell stories work in prose, in full-length novels or short stories, or in scripts for stage or screen. It is hard to imagine a time when novels did not exist but they first appear in the mid-seventeenth century. These first novels – often called 'histories' – mainly dealt with romances of illicit love. Gradually, novelists tackled more and more subjects. By the late eighteenth century the novel was the dominant form for most types of storytelling and it remains so today.

Verse narratives suited an audience such as Chaucer's, most of whom were illiterate and would have listened to *The Canterbury Tales* being read aloud. The regular ten-syllable line lengths and the end rhymes set up a rhythmic pattern which helps the story along when spoken aloud.

CHECK THE BOOK

The poet Andrew Waterman wrote a long sequence of 178 identically structured fourteen-line poems, creating a verse autobiography, in his book *Out For The Elements* (Carcanet Press, 1981). It is a lively and at times funny set of poems.

CHECK THE BOOK

The chief novelists of the eighteenth century, in the period when the modern novel form was being developed, were Daniel Defoe (*Robinson Crusoe*, 1719), Samuel Richardson (*Pamela*, 1740), Henry Fielding (*Tom Jones*, 1749) and Tobias Smollett (*The Adventures of Roderick Random*, 1748).

The ten syllable iambic line of heroic couplet became the core structural device of English narrative verse for centuries after Chaucer, and its variant, unrhymed iambic blank verse, became the standard measure of Elizabethan and later drama. The iambic form is not such a complex structure that the writer has to spend all his time working out how to fit what he want to say into it. It can accommodate, as in *The Canterbury Tales* and in all Shakespeare's plays, the 'voices' of different characters. Its regular pattern allows writers to explore complex ideas and thoughts, and this rhythm gives vigour to the expression of intellectual ideas, as is shown by the Pardoner's lengthy sermon against various sins. The fixed rhythm makes complex ideas easier to follow. Unlike modern poetry, which often uses complex imagery, metaphors and similes which reveal their full meaning only after re-reading, iambic verse narratives can be a frame to express ideas with directness and energy.

CHAUCER AND OTHER WRITERS

Chaucer is the earliest writer in English to have left us a large and diverse body of written work. The only other major English language text written before Chaucer is *Beowulf*, an anonymous poem dealing with mythic themes probably written in the eighth century, surviving in a tenth century manuscript. It is written in Old English (as opposed to Chaucer's Middle English).

Chaucer's works have influenced many later writers, but because he was writing so early in the canon of English literature he does not appear himself to have been influenced by many other – or perhaps any other – English creative writers. His influences were French, Italian, and classical authors writing in Latin such as Ovid, Virgil and Petrarch.

There are very few writers of fiction in English who predate him or who are contemporary with him. Only two major narrative poems survive from Medieval England. William Langland's *Piers Plowman* appeared in or around1370, but Langland deals much more with allegorical form and figures, while Chaucer, though there are elements of allegory in many of the Tales, is ultimately the supreme early writer who reflects the human condition in all its forms. *Sir Gawain and the Green Knight* (1375–1400?) is a lengthy anonymous romance in the Arthurian tradition. There is only one

CONTEXT

Ovid (43 BC–AD 18), was a Roman poet exiled by the Emperor Augustus. He wrote a number of **elegiac** poems and was the favourite Latin poet of the Middle Ages. Virgil's (70–12 BC) chief work is *The Aeneid*, an epic historical poem, dramatising the adventures of Aeneas and his Trojans. Petrarch (1304–74) was an Italian poet, best known for being a great humanist and patriot.

manuscript surviving from the period of its composition. The author is referred to as 'The Pearl Poet' and is thought to have composed two shorter poems which are included in the manuscript, *Cleanness* and *Patience*. Like *Piers Plowman*, *Sir Gawain and the Green Knight* is a formalised and courtly work that lacks the variety of style and subject, reality and humanity of *The Canterbury Tales*.

Chaucer would have drawn on a number of written sources for the material that went into *The Canterbury Tales*. Some of these, like the folk tale that forms the core of *The Pardoner's Tale*, are barely recorded as they come from an oral tradition. We can trace much more easily the French and Italian authors he read, translated and was influenced by. Most of the references that Chaucer uses in *The Pardoner's Tale* are to non-fiction texts, such as the writings of the first century AD Roman writer-philosopher Seneca, and the Bible and Christian theological treatises for the many religious references. (See **Detailed Summaries** and **Language and style: Allusion** for discussion of these.)

CHECK THE NET
The University of Glasgow has a webpage called 'The World of Chaucer' which displays facsimile pages from a 1476 manuscript, and a variety of early printed versions – the 1526 edition includes a woodblock of the Pardoner. Go to **www.special.lib.gla.ac.uk** and click on 'Exhibitions'.

HISTORICAL BACKGROUND

PILGRIMAGES

The idea of demonstrating religious devotion by making a journey of pilgrimage to a shrine or holy site was a core part of the practices of the Catholic Church in Chaucer's time. Catholics (and other Christian denominations to a lesser extent) still make pilgrimages to places where miraculous healing might take place, for example Lourdes in France and Walsingham in Norfolk. However, most Christians today do not regard a pilgrimage as an essential duty, unlike the Haj or pilgrimage to Mecca which is an important part of the Muslim faith. In Chaucer's day, pilgrimages were made to various shrines around England. The ultimate, and most dangerous, pilgrimage to make, however, was to the Holy Land (modern Israel) to visit places mentioned in the Bible.

Of the various pilgrimages that people could quite easily undertake to destinations in England, one of the most popular was a journey to worship at the shrine of the martyr St Thomas à Becket in Canterbury Cathedral. To pray at the shrine was considered of great

PILGRIMAGES continued

Pilgrimages to sites in the Holy Land were not often possible in the Middle Ages because much of it was occupied by Arab armies which had invaded several centuries before Chaucer's time. This had resulted in the Crusades, which, unlike peaceful pilgrimages, were military expeditions to the Holy Land to wrest back control of biblical sites.

benefit and a religious experience. The journey from London would take a few days on a horse progressing at a gentle trot. Chaucer's aim of two days each way seems a bit optimistic as it is fifty-nine miles between London and Canterbury, following rough tracks.

Pilgrims would gather at inns in London that offered accommodation, and strangers formed groups for companionship and support along the way. Chaucer's pilgrims gather at the Tabard Inn, which stood on what is now Borough High Street, just south of the River Thames and the Tate Modern art gallery on Bankside in Southwark. This is close to the Canterbury Road, and the exact site of the inn is marked by a plaque on the wall of the building that now stands there.

Although there was some possible danger along the roads from robbers – and as the Pardoner points out as part of his 'sales pitch' at the end of the tale, the danger of being thrown from your horse and killed was always present – as medieval pilgrimages went, London to Canterbury was a fairly safe and easy one. Chaucer's pilgrims are travelling in the spring, so even have a fair chance of enjoying good weather. For more rigorous believers, a worthwhile pilgrimage had to involve some degree of hardship to test their religious convictions, and it has been suggested that Chaucer was implying, by his choice of a spring journey to Canterbury, that this group of pilgrims were fairly relaxed and easy going; that they had waited until the winter and its potential hardships had passed. Nowhere in *The Canterbury Tales* are any really zealous views about the holiness of their journey expressed by any pilgrim, though most of course express heartfelt religious convictions. Indeed, once they have got underway and the Tales start to be told, it is easy to forget, as they themselves often appear to do, that this is a journey driven by a holy purpose. They amble along swapping stories, laughing a lot and stopping, as at the start of *The Pardoner's Prologue*, in roadside ale houses. They often avow religious convictions, of course, and they admire the Wife of Bath for her previous pilgrimages, but none of them appears too committed to a sober religious experience on the road to Canterbury. It almost appears an extended social outing, and of course it provides a wonderful frame for Chaucer to build his stories around.

PARDONERS AND THE TREASURY OF GRACE

Punishment and absolution for sins was a core part of the teachings of the Catholic Church in Chaucer's time. Penances had to be fulfilled to atone for all forms of wrong-doing. Repeating prayers or fasting were common penances. Gradually the practice of allowing sinners to give alms (money) to the Church instead of performing a penance took hold.

About a century before *The Canterbury Tales* were written, the Church developed a theory called 'The Treasury of Grace'. This said that the Church guarded a great store of goodness or 'merits' created by God and all his saints. These were more than enough to balance out all the sins that mankind would ever commit, and so the Church could distribute merits to its members – for a fee. All that a sinner had to do was be truly repentant and, of course, give money. Thus people did not have perform actual penances and the Church obtained money to do its work.

Special officers were created to do the work of distributing or selling what came to be known as 'pardons'. These officers were called *quaestores* in Latin – the language the Church used in all its official business and services – or, in English, pardoners. These could be priests or monks, or, like our Pardoner, they could be a lay person employed by the Church. The idea was that they would be carefully regulated by the Church and would be given a letter of authorisation from a high-ranking churchman, often a bishop, which was in effect the pardoner's licence to operate. They gave the money they collected from congregations who bought pardons to the Church, keeping back a small agreed amount for themselves.

Not surprisingly, the system quickly went wrong. By the time Chaucer was writing *The Canterbury Tales* the whole system was regarded by many people as pure fraud. The Pardoner in *The Canterbury Tales* is a corrupt figure who many of Chaucer's readers would recognise. Chaucer is not specifically creating a **satirical** anti-church figure, but describes a character that was all too common in daily life at the end of the fourteenth century.

 CHECK THE NET

The Luminarium website, **http://www. luminarium.org/** contains notes on *The Pardoner's Tale* and useful links to more specialised articles and papers on aspects of the work. This site can provide you with useful further reading to expand your understanding of the social, cultural and religious context in which Chaucer wrote.

CHECK THE NET
See the British Library website, **www.bl.uk/treasures**, for an account of how William Caxton printed indulgences for sale in 1476, coincidentally the same year as he printed his first edition of *The Canterbury Tales*. Search for 'Caxton pardoners'.

There were not many other writers working in Chaucer's lifetime (or if there were, their works have been lost) and it is interesting that one of them also drew an unflattering picture of fraudulent pardoners. In his poem *Piers Plowman* (which appeared in three version between 1362 and 1392), William Langland describes how a pardoner preached like a priest, although they were forbidden to do so. He describes 'ignorant' men coming forward on their knees to kiss the pardoner's licence. The pardoner pushes his letters of indulgence – the document by which he absolves them of their sins – into their faces and takes their rings and brooches as payment. Unlike Chaucer, Langland doesn't actually say his pardoner is a fraud, but his description is of a rapacious, money-grabbing man. If the two greatest writers of the age both portrayed pardoners as frauds and villains, we can safely assume that was how many of their readers regarded them.

HOLY RELICS

Relics were (and still are to some Catholics) miracle-working objects that could be worshipped, sold to individuals or, if they were considered exceptionally rare, be bought by a church to draw pilgrims to it. At the great Catholic shrine at Walsingham in Norfolk, for example, a phial said to contain some of the Virgin Mary's breast milk was once displayed to pilgrims. Kissing relics was a way of gaining the powers they supposedly contained. Our pilgrims are heading for the shrine of St Thomas in Canterbury Cathedral where one of the relics they were encouraged to kiss were the hair breeches which the saint wore next to his skin, as a form of self-punishment.

The medieval Church saw spiritual power as existing in material objects in a way that we find hard to understand today. The Christian world was full of relics supposed to have been in contact with the saints, or were believed to have been an actual part of their body. Many were fake. There are currently approximately twenty-nine nails held by Christian institutions around the world from the 'true cross' on which Jesus was supposedly crucified.

Historical Background	Chaucer's Life	Literary Background
1170 Thomas à Becket murdered in Canterbury Cathedral (canonised in 1173)		
1300 Population of British Isles around five million		
1309 Papal See moves to Avignon and comes under French control		
1313 Death of Jean de Meun, author of part two of *Roman de la Rose*, allegorical poem mocking love, women, the Church and those in authority		
		1319 Death of Jean de Joinville, French chronicler
1321 Edward II forced to abdicate, imprisoned and probably murdered; Edward III accedes to throne, with wife Philippa		**1321** Death of Dante Alighieri, author of *The Divine Comedy*
		1330 Birth of John Gower, poet and friend of Chaucer
		1331 Birth of William Langland, poet
		1337 Birth of Jean Froissart, who will become clerk of the Chamber to Queen Philippa and author of *Chronicles*, a history of fourteenth century western Europe and the code of chivalry
1338 Beginning of the Hundred Years War between France and England		

Historical Background	Chaucer's Life	Literary Background
	1343 or 4 Birth of Geoffrey Chaucer in London	1341 Petrarch crowned as laureate poet in the Capitol, Rome
1346 French routed at Crecy by Edward III and his son the Black Prince		
1349 Black Death reaches England and kills one third of the population		
		c. 1350 *Mary Magdalen*, Saints play
1351 First Statute of Labourers regulates wages in England		
		1353 In Italy, Giovanni Boccaccio finishes his *Decameron*, a collection of a hundred tales
1356 English defeat the French at Poitiers		
	1357 Chaucer in the service of the Countess of Ulster, wife of Prince Lionel, third son of Edward III	
1359 Edward III makes unsuccessful bid for French throne	1359 Serves in the army in France, under Prince Lionel; taken prisoner	
1360 France cedes a number of territories to England	1360 Edward III pays ransom of £16 for Chaucer's freedom	

Historical Background	Chaucer's Life	Literary Background
1361 Black Death reappears in England		
1362 English becomes official language in Parliament and the Law Courts		**1363** Birth of Christine de Pisan, French author of *La Cité des Dames*, listing all the heroic acts and virtues of woman
	1366 Marries Philippa Pan (or Payne) Roet; in Spain on a diplomatic mission	
	1367 Granted life pension for his services to the king; birth of his son Thomas; begins travelling abroad on the king's business	
	1368 On Prince Lionel's death, his services transferred to John of Gaunt, Duke of Lancaster	
	1369 In Picardy with John of Gaunt's expeditionary force; begins *The Book of the Duchess* on the death of Blanche, John of Gaunt's wife	
	1370–3 Sent on diplomatic missions to Genoa and Florence	**1370** (c.) William Langland's *Piers Plowman* (first version)
	1374 Appointed Controller of the Customs and Subsidy of Wools, Skins and Hides; receives a life pension from John of Gaunt	

Historical Background	Chaucer's Life	Literary Background
		1375 (c.) *Sir Gawain and the Green Knight* written (anonymously)
	1376 Receives payment for some secret, unspecified service	
1377 Edward III dies and is succeeded by Richard II, son of the Black Prince	1377 Employed on secret missions to Flanders, and sent to France to negotiate for peace with Charles V	
1378 Beginning of the Great Schism; Urban VI elected Pope in Rome, Clement VII in Avignon	1378 On diplomatic mission to the Lord of Milan	
1380 John Wyclif, who attacked orthodox Church doctrines, condemned as a heretic; Wyclif's followers translate Bible into vernacular Middle English; civil authorities in London issue warrants for the arrest of persons claiming to be collecting alms for the Hospital of Our Lady of Rouncivale	1380 *Parliament of Fowls* written; birth of son Louis. Cecilia Chaumpayne releases Chaucer from a charge of '*de raptu meo*'	1380s Religious and 'Mystery' plays popular at this time
1381 Peasants' Revolt under Wat Tyler quelled by Richard II		
	1382 Appointed Controller of the Petty Customs	
	1385 Appoints deputy to perform his duties as Controller; writing *Legend of Good Women* and *Troilus and Criseyde*; living in Greenwich	

Historical Background	Chaucer's Life	Literary Background
1386 Richard II deprived of power	1386 Deprived of both official posts; elected a Knight of the Shire of Kent **Chaucer's Life**	
	1387 Wife Philippa dies; begins writing *The Canterbury Tales*	
	1388 Chaucer sell his pensions to raise money	
1389 Richard II resumes power	1389 Appointed Clerk of King's Works and becomes deputy forester of the royal forest at North Petherton, Somerset	
1390 Pope Boniface IX issues a letter warning against false pardoners		1390 Gower's *Confession*
1396 John of Gaunt, Duke of Lancaster, marries his mistress, Katherine de Roet, Chaucer's sister-in-law		
1399 Richard II forced to abdicate; Henry IV becomes king of England		
1400 Richard II dies in prison; population of British Isles around three and a half million	1400 Death of Chaucer	1400 Arthurian verse romances

TRANSLATIONS

You may find it useful to read a contemporary retelling or 'translation' of Chaucer's text of *The Pardoner's Tale* in modern English. Two versions of the complete *Canterbury Tales* are suggested here, but neither will contain a text that will correspond line by line, let alone word for word, with the Cambridge edition original text on which these Notes are based. The interlinear version of selected tales (below) may be a better choice for reading a modern version of *The Pardoner's Tale*:

Nevill Coghill, *Chaucer: The Canterbury Tales*, Penguin, most recent edition, 2003
A classic verse translation

Vincent Hooper, *Chaucer's Canterbury Tales, An Interlinear Translation*, Barron's Educational Series, 1963
Selected Tales, including *The Pardoner's Tale*, printed in Middle English with a line by line modern English version interwoven. (This can help you speed up your reading of Middle English)

David Wright, *Chaucer: The Canterbury Tales*, Oxford University Press, 1964
A prose translation

BACKGROUND AND LITERARY CRITICISM: *THE PARDONER'S TALE* AND *THE CANTERBURY TALES*

The following books can provide you with in-depth background and further reading to support your understanding of the text and its social, literary and historical context.

Peter Ackroyd, *Chaucer (Brief Lives)*, Vintage, 2005
A very readable account of Chaucer's life and works

Gail Ashton, *Chaucer: The Canterbury Tales*, Palgrave-Macmillan, 1998
Contains a number of general approaches to a critical study of the text

Barber, Leone, Nardo and Siebold, (Editors), *Readings on The Canterbury Tales*, Greenhaven Press, 1997
Contains large sections on Chaucer's language and verse, themes and characterisation

Ian Bishop, *The Narrative Art of The Canterbury Tales*, Dent, 1987
Looks in detail at how Chaucer constructs the key narratives in the Tales

FURTHER READING

Lillian Bisson, *Chaucer and the Late Medieval World*, Palgrave-Macmillan, 1998

> Examines key social issues that influence Chaucer's work

Harold Bloom, *The Pardoner's Tale: Bloom's Modern Critical Interpretations*, Chelsea House Publications, 2000

> Bloom is a world renowned Shakespeare scholar who here turns his critical attentions to considering diverse readings of the Tale

Boitani and Mann (Editors), *The Cambridge Chaucer Companion*, Cambridge University Press, 1986

> A good range of general information on the Tales

Derek Brewer, *Chaucer and his World*, Boydell and Brewer, 1978

> Uses a lot of visual imagery to produce a broad picture of Chaucer's world

D. S. Brewer, *Geoffrey Chaucer; Writers and their Background*, University of Toronto Press, 1974

> Brewer is one of the best and most prolific contemporary Chaucer scholars and here he places *The Canterbury Tales* in their historical context

Helen Cooper, *Oxford Guide to Chaucer: The Canterbury Tales*, Oxford University Press, 1989

> A good introduction to the sources and historical background to *The Canterbury Tales*

Stephen Knight and Terry Eagelton, *Geoffrey Chaucer*, Blackwell, 1986

> Classic Marxist critical interpretation of Chaucer's work

Anna Laskaya, *Chaucer's Approach to Gender in The Canterbury Tales*, Cambridge University Press, 1995

> In-depth study of Chaucer's attitudes to gender and male/female roles

Jill Mann, *Chaucer and Medieval Estates Satire: The Literature of Social Class and The General Prologue to The Canterbury Tales*, Cambridge University Press, 1973

> Detailed study suggesting the pilgrims are satirical examples of the characters from estate satire

Jill Mann, *Feminising Chaucer*, Boydell and Brewer, 2002

> Reviews Chaucer's handling of gender issues misogynistic stereotypes

Paul Olson, *The Canterbury Tales and the Good Society*, Princetown, 1986
  Detailed analysis of social issues in *The Canterbury Tales*

Derek Pearsell, *The Life of Geoffrey Chaucer*, Blackwell, 1992
  A detailed critical biography of Chaucer

Helen Philips, *An Introduction to The Canterbury Tales: Reading, Fiction and Context*, Palgrave-Macmillan, 1999
  Good general overview of the Tales, locating individual tales into the work's overall frame

Gillian Rudd, *Complete Critical Guide to Chaucer*, Routledge, 2001
  A detailed critical overview of all Chaucer's works

WIDER READING

GOTHIC TEXTS

Emily Bronte, *Wuthering Heights*, 1847

Angela Carter, *The Bloody Chamber*, 1979

Daphne du Maurier, *Jamaica Inn*, 1936

Christopher Marlowe, *Dr Faustus*, 1604

John Milton, *Paradise Lost, Books I and II*, 1667

William Shakespeare, *Macbeth*, 1603

Mary Shelley, *Frankenstein*, 1818

Bram Stoker, *Dracula*, 1897

Horace Walpole, *The Castle of Otranto; A Gothic Story*, 1769

John Webster, *The White Devil* and *The Duchess of Malfi*, 1612 and 1614

VERSE NARRATIVES

John Bunyan, *The Pilgrim's Progress*, 1678

William Langland, *Piers Plowman*, (written circa 1360–99)

Andrew Waterman, *Out For The Elements*, Carcanet Press, 1981

EARLY NOVELS

Daniel Defoe, *Robinson Crusoe*, 1719

Henry Fielding, *Tom Jones*, 1749

Samuel Richardson, *Pamela*, 1740

Tobias Smollett, *The Adventures of Roderick Random*, 1748

allusions (classical) references to characters and events from classical stories and tales, and from myths and legends (especially Greek myths)

acrostic a poem in which the first or last letters of certain lines, when read in order, spell a word or phrase, or work through the alphabet

allegory a story or a situation with two different meanings, where the straightforward meaning on the surface is used to symbolise a deeper meaning underneath. This secondary meaning is often a spiritual or moral one whose values are represented by specific figures, characters or events in the narrative

alliteration the repetition of the same consonant or a sequence of vowels in a stretch of language, most often at the beginnings of words or on stressed syllables

allusion a passing reference in a work of literature to something outside the text; may include other works of literature, myth, historical facts or biographical detail

aphorism a generally accepted truth or principle expressed in a short, pithy way

ballad originally lyrics to be sung, ballads developed into a style of poem constructed in short verses usually dealing with popular themes

blank verse unrhymed iambic pentameter

colloquial the everyday speech used by people in informal situations

courtly romance a stylised love story played out to a set of chivalric and usually morally and spiritually high-flown rules

dramatisation the turning of one form of story – fact or fiction – into a work for performance

denouement the final unravelling of a plot in a drama

dialogue direct speech between two or more characters in a text

didactic literature designed to instruct or inform

elegiac generally, a style of reflective poetry which features the presence of the poet in some way. In a stricter sense, an elegy is a poem or song lamenting the dead

estate satires comic critical stories featuring a cast of characters representative of different occupations and social standings, popular in the Middle Ages

farce stage plays written purely for comic effect, usually involving misunderstanding and social embarrassment of characters

genre a collective grouping of a type of prose, poetry, story or play

gothic literature a style of writing characterised by a gloomy atmosphere and a focus on the macabre

heroic couplet a pair of rhyming **iambic pentameters**. First developed by Chaucer, this became the basic poetic measure of much early English poetry and some early stage drama

iambic pentameter a ten syllable line of poetry consisting of five iambic feet (iambic consisting of a weak syllable followed by a strong one)

imagery, images figurative language referring to objects or qualities in a way that is designed to evoke a particular emotive or intellectual response

interlinear translation an original text in one language with a parallel translation into another added line by line

metaphor a figure of speech in which a word or phrase is applied to an object, a character or an action which does not literally belong to it, in order to imply a resemblance and create an unusual or striking image in the reader's mind

misogyny a negative attitude to women

moral tale a tale or narrative designed to illustrate a moral truth

onomatopoeia the use of words whose sounds echo the noises they describe

pathos writing or speech that gives the effect of pity or sadness

personification the treatment or description of an object or an idea as human, with human attributes and feelings

revenge tragedies a genre of violent and usually simplistic stories in which a wrong has to be avenged

rhetoric the art of writing or speaking persuasively

rhetorical question a question asked by a speaker to an audience that is designed to make them think but not actually reply

rhyming couplet two lines of verse of equal metrical length whose endings rhyme with one another

Saints plays popular plays of the early Middle Ages, using the life of a 'merry' (as opposed, for example, to a horribly martyred) saint as the basis of a generally light-hearted drama

satire a type of literature in which folly, evil or topical issues are held up to scorn through ridicule, irony or exaggeration

scatological a bawdy or obscene word or expression

sermon a speech focused on promoting some religious truth or point of doctrine given in a church by a minister

synonym a word that means the same or nearly the same as another word

thematic the abstract idea of a work

Shaun McCarthy is a playwright, poet and author of educational resources. His stage plays have been produced at Bristol Old Vic and the Actor's Centre, Covent Garden. He has had original plays and Classic Serial adaptations produced on BBC Radio 3 and Radio 4. He has published over twenty education resource books on English Literature, Drama and contemporary and historical biographies. He teaches creative writing as visiting playwright at Oxford and Bristol universities.

NOTES

GCSE

Maya Angelou
I Know Why the Caged Bird Sings

Jane Austen
Pride and Prejudice

Alan Ayckbourn
Absent Friends

Elizabeth Barrett Browning
Selected Poems

Robert Bolt
A Man for All Seasons

Harold Brighouse
Hobson's Choice

Charlotte Brontë
Jane Eyre

Emily Brontë
Wuthering Heights

Brian Clark
Whose Life is it Anyway?

Robert Cormier
Heroes

Shelagh Delaney
A Taste of Honey

Charles Dickens
David Copperfield
Great Expectations
Hard Times
Oliver Twist
Selected Stories

Roddy Doyle
Paddy Clarke Ha Ha Ha

George Eliot
Silas Marner
The Mill on the Floss

Anne Frank
The Diary of a Young Girl

William Golding
Lord of the Flies

Oliver Goldsmith
She Stoops to Conquer

Willis Hall
The Long and the Short and the Tall

Thomas Hardy
Far from the Madding Crowd
The Mayor of Casterbridge
Tess of the d'Urbervilles
The Withered Arm and other Wessex Tales

L. P. Hartley
The Go-Between

Seamus Heaney
Selected Poems

Susan Hill
I'm the King of the Castle

Barry Hines
A Kestrel for a Knave

Louise Lawrence
Children of the Dust

Harper Lee
To Kill a Mockingbird

Laurie Lee
Cider with Rosie

Arthur Miller
The Crucible
A View from the Bridge

Robert O'Brien
Z for Zachariah

Frank O'Connor
My Oedipus Complex and Other Stories

George Orwell
Animal Farm

J.B. Priestley
An Inspector Calls
When We Are Married

Willy Russell
Educating Rita
Our Day Out

J. D. Salinger
The Catcher in the Rye

William Shakespeare
Henry IV Part I
Henry V
Julius Caesar
Macbeth
The Merchant of Venice
A Midsummer Night's Dream
Much Ado About Nothing
Romeo and Juliet
The Tempest
Twelfth Night

George Bernard Shaw
Pygmalion

Mary Shelley
Frankenstein

R.C. Sherriff
Journey's End

Rukshana Smith
Salt on the snow

John Steinbeck
Of Mice and Men

Robert Louis Stevenson
Dr Jekyll and Mr Hyde

Jonathan Swift
Gulliver's Travels

Robert Swindells
Daz 4 Zoe

Mildred D. Taylor
Roll of Thunder, Hear My Cry

Mark Twain
Huckleberry Finn

James Watson
Talking in Whispers

Edith Wharton
Ethan Frome

William Wordsworth
Selected Poems

A Choice of Poets

Mystery Stories of the Nineteenth Century including The Signalman

Nineteenth Century Short Stories

Poetry of the First World War

Six Women Poets

For the AQA Anthology:

Duffy and Armitage & Pre-1914 Poetry

Heaney and Clarke & Pre-1914 Poetry

Poems from Different Cultures

Key Stage 3

William Shakespeare
Henry V
Macbeth
Much Ado About Nothing
Richard III
The Tempest

Margaret Atwood
Cat's Eye
The Handmaid's Tale

Jane Austen
Emma
Mansfield Park
Persuasion
Pride and Prejudice
Sense and Sensibility

William Blake
Songs of Innocence and of Experience

The Brontës
Selected Poems

Charlotte Brontë
Jane Eyre
Villette

Emily Brontë
Wuthering Heights

Angela Carter
The Bloody Chamber
Nights at the Circus
Wise Children

Geoffrey Chaucer
The Franklin's Prologue and Tale
The Merchant's Prologue and Tale
The Miller's Prologue and Tale
The Pardoner's Tale
The Prologue to the Canterbury Tales
The Wife of Bath's Prologue and Tale

Caryl Churchill
Top Girls

John Clare
Selected Poems

Joseph Conrad
Heart of Darkness

Charles Dickens
Bleak House
Great Expectations
Hard Times

Emily Dickinson
Selected Poems

Carol Ann Duffy
Selected Poems
The World's Wife

George Eliot
Middlemarch
The Mill on the Floss

T. S. Eliot
Selected Poems
The Waste Land

F. Scott Fitzgerald
The Great Gatsby

John Ford
'Tis Pity She's a Whore

Michael Frayn
Spies

Charles Frazier
Cold Mountain

Brian Friel
Making History
Translations

William Golding
The Spire

Thomas Hardy
Jude the Obscure
The Mayor of Casterbridge
The Return of the Native
Selected Poems
Tess of the d'Urbervilles

Nathaniel Hawthorne
The Scarlet Letter

Seamus Heaney
Selected Poems from 'Opened Ground'

Homer
The Iliad
The Odyssey

Aldous Huxley
Brave New World

Henrik Ibsen
A Doll's House

Kazuo Ishiguro
The Remains of the Day

James Joyce
Dubliners

John Keats
Selected Poems

Philip Larkin
High Windows
The Whitsun Weddings and Selected Poems

Ian McEwan
Atonement

Christopher Marlowe
Doctor Faustus
Edward II

Arthur Miller
All My Sons
Death of a Salesman

John Milton
Paradise Lost Books I & II

Toni Morrison
Beloved

George Orwell
Nineteen Eighty-Four

Sylvia Plath
Selected Poems

William Shakespeare
Antony and Cleopatra
As You Like It
Hamlet
Henry IV Part I
King Lear
Macbeth
Measure for Measure
The Merchant of Venice
A Midsummer Night's Dream
Much Ado About Nothing
Othello
Richard II
Richard III
Romeo and Juliet
The Taming of the Shrew
The Tempest
Twelfth Night
The Winter's Tale

Mary Shelley
Frankenstein

Richard Brinsley Sheridan
The School for Scandal

Bram Stoker
Dracula

Alfred Tennyson
Selected Poems

Alice Walker
The Color Purple

John Webster
The Duchess of Malfi
The White Devil

Oscar Wilde
The Importance of Being Earnest
A Woman of No Importance

Tennessee Williams
Cat on a Hot Tin Roof
The Glass Menagerie
A Streetcar Named Desire

Jeanette Winterson
Oranges Are Not the Only Fruit

Virginia Woolf
To the Lighthouse

William Wordsworth
The Prelude and Selected Poems

W. B. Yeats
Selected Poems

Poetry of the First World War